THE
LEAST
OF
THESE

**ONE MAN'S REMARKABLE
JOURNEY IN THE FIGHT
AGAINST CHILD TRAFFICKING**

JEFF BRODSKY

INTERNATIONAL

Published by JOY International
Conifer, Colorado, USA
www.joy.org
Printed in the USA

ISBN-13: 978-0-9993941-0-6

Disclaimer: Some names and identifying details have been changed
to protect the privacy of individuals.

Cover design by Pear Creative
Interior design by InsideOut CreativeArts

DEDICATION

As of this writing, my remarkable wife, Gail, and I have been married for forty-three years. The words "separation" and "divorce" have never entered our vocabulary. Not once. Simply put, today we are more in love with each other than ever before.

Our commitment runs deep, but that doesn't mean we agree on everything. Just the reverse is true. We could be the poster couple for the adage "opposites attract."

How each of us feels about pets illustrates my point. If I had my druthers, our home would be completely animal free. No stray hairs, no yapping, no potty training. But we have horses and dogs for one reason: Gail enjoys them. Happy wife, happy life! Gail's even become a champion canine freestyle doggy dancer. Yes, she performs competitive dancing with her dogs.

Fighting against the commercial sexual exploitation of children often takes me out of town. While I am gone, the animals are great companions for her. I am happy she has them to keep her company, but this highlights another difference between her and me: I relish going to faraway places; Gail does not. If she never boarded a plane again, she'd be ecstatic.

As part of my work, I tell my story to myriad groups. A few years ago I was invited to speak at a women's conference in Colorado. While Gail doesn't like to travel, she does love to hear me talk about my work. Since this particular event was only forty-five minutes from our house, she joined me.

When I speak, I get into a groove. I was rolling along that day, about halfway into my narrative, when a woman in the audience interrupted me.

"Excuse me. May I ask you a question?"

I was a little surprised but nodded.

"Let me see if I understand you correctly," she said. "Are you saying that you go undercover into brothels, and at times the girls you meet will be sexually aggressive?"

"Yes," I responded, "but I always firmly tell the girls, 'No touching!'"

The woman pressed on.

"And you're married?"

"Yes, I am—*very* happily married."

"And your wife approves of this?"

"Yes, she does. If she didn't, I wouldn't do it."

"I don't understand," she said, shaking her head. "How can your wife allow you to go into brothels?"

I had not yet introduced Gail, so the group had no clue she was present.

"That's a great question," I said. "It just so happens that this is one of those rare times when my wife, Gail, is with me. Hon, can you come up here?"

An uncertain look on Gail's face telegraphed just how nervous she was. She doesn't like to speak in public. Nevertheless, she rose from her seat and walked forward. Not knowing exactly what she would say, I handed her the microphone. You could hear the proverbial pin drop as she began.

"I trust Jeff completely," she told the group. "I know he listens when God speaks to him, and I believe him when he says God called him to do this.

"I also know my husband's heart. I know exactly what he sees when he sees one of these girls. He doesn't see a prostitute; he sees the face of his daughter. He sees the face of his granddaughter—and he would give his life to set her free.

"I'm called to support him in his work and to pray for him when he's on a rescue mission. I pray every day for direction, guidance and wisdom—and I pray especially for God's protection over my husband. I'm very proud of the work God has called him to do. Besides, what kind of wife would I be if I denied the calling God has placed on Jeff's life?"

I swallowed a lump as she went back to her seat.

I could not and would not do the work I do without Gail's full love and support. The love I have for her is truly immeasurable. It is to this precious woman of God and the love of my life that I dedicate this book.

CONTENTS

PREFACE

I am just a Jewish guy who looks like Santa Claus and has lots of life stories to tell.

In 2010 I took off my shoes and socks, and I have not put them back on since. Every day of every week, 365 days a year, everywhere I go, I go barefoot. In this book I tell how I became shoeless (and sockless) and why I will remain that way for the rest of my life. But for now, suffice it to say that I go barefoot as a demonstration of solidarity with impoverished children around the world, specifically those who are at risk of child sex trafficking.

I have spent twelve years fighting to rescue these children and raise awareness about their plight. This book shares what I've seen while fighting the horrible industry of child sex trafficking, which only seems to get bigger every year. My sole purpose for writing this book (and sharing some deeply personal experiences) is to move you and everyone who will join me on my journey to action. It is filled with stories and motivating facts that I pray will stir your heart and move you to get involved in the fight to bring justice to the lowest of the low. One voice can be strong, but is it enough to make a difference?

Throughout Scripture God expresses His desire for us to champion the oppressed. One day as I was reading the red words in my Bible (words spoken directly by Jesus), I was gripped by what Jesus said about helping those He called "the least of these":

> The King will say to those on His right hand, "Come, you blessed of My Father, inherit the kingdom prepared for

you from the foundation of the world: for I was hungry and you gave Me food; I was thirsty and you gave Me drink; I was a stranger and you took Me in; I was naked and you clothed Me; I was sick and you visited Me; I was in prison and you came to Me."

Then the righteous will answer Him, saying, "Lord, when did we see You hungry and feed You, or thirsty and give You drink? When did we see You a stranger and take You in, or naked and clothe You? Or when did we see You sick, or in prison, and come to You?" And the King will answer and say to them, "Assuredly, I say to you, inasmuch as you did it to one of *the least of these* My brethren, you did it to Me." (Matthew 25:34–40)

There is no better example of one who bears the yoke of oppression than a child sex slave.

You may remember Dr. Seuss's beloved classic *Horton Hears a Who!* While trying to save their city from destruction, the citizens of Whoville made as much noise as they possibly could, but they were not loud enough for the big kangaroo to hear them. When the mayor eventually found the shirker, the city was saved because they had finally all worked together.

Are you a shirker? My guess is that you're not. Why would you be reading this book otherwise? But if we do shirk our responsibility and duty to innocent children, then we are complicit in their pain and suffering. I know that's harsh. But if you read this book and choose to do nothing except be aware, then their blood is on your hands.

Change will require each of us to see this injustice and then *take action* to make a difference in the life of a child's endless horror. Compassion is only compassion when we do something. Like Jesus' parable of the good Samaritan, we must cross the road to rescue and restore the wounded. It's not enough to feel sad or disgusted by evil. Compassion requires action. No matter who we are, what country we live in, or what language we speak, we must all cry out in unison to *end* the evil against our children.

Will you join me? Alone I can do little. But when we raise our voices together, we can change the world for millions of children who are desperately crying out and begging for help. How will that happen? Keep reading. I'll tell you soon enough.

You are God's hands, yet He cannot do much through you without your obedience and compassion. I believe that as you read the stories in this book, you'll become more than a hearer—you'll become a doer.

I like the quote commonly attributed to Irish philosopher Edmund Burke: "The only thing necessary for the triumph of evil is for good men to do nothing." I have my own adage: awareness without action is apathy.

Thank you for going on this journey with me. I pray that you will be changed as you take Jesus' red letters to head and heart.

ACKNOWLEDGMENTS

With so many years representing my life in these pages, I want to personally thank the following people and organizations for their contributions to my inspiration and knowledge and other help in creating this book. Without them this book would never have been completed.

This book would never have come to life without my entire (and incredible) publishing team! My project director and editors Steve and Becky Lawson, you are the best. It's been a long journey, but I'll never be able to thank you both enough for bringing this book to life! Also assisting with the writing and editing were Steve Laube, Lindy Lowry, and Brad and Grant Rahme. Thank you also to proofreader Jennifer Cullis, cover designer Yvonne Parks, interior designer Rob Williams, and e-book designer Jason Chatraw.

Pat and Robin Davis (Pat, if I had a dollar for every minute we spent together talking about this book, I would never have to raise funds again); Pastor Lance Swearengin (it's finished, now leave me alone); Wendy Francisco, thank you for the many hours of your wisdom and heart; Dale Hammitt, my dear friend and Alaskan brother and my home away from home, you provided the perfect sanctuary for me to write; Lynda Chud, my Alaskan sister, for your love and friendship (still praying).

The following families and churches for years of generous support and encouragement: the Pepperd family; Jon and Michelle Abbott; Cornerstone Wesleyan Church in Kansas City, Missouri (with a shout out to Jean Ann Rucker and Sheralyn Smith and the entire Cornerstone family); Pastor Peter Young and BridgeWay

Church in Denver; Platte Canyon Community Church in Bailey, Colorado; and Pastor Ryan Paulson and the entire South Fellowship in Littleton, Colorado; and too many churches around the world to mention!

For my special friends and board members who gave constant encouragement and support: Greg Blake, Terry Rogers, Katy Moses, Dave Smith (my friend and Web guru). Also, I could not run JOY International without my incredible staff of Gina Moran, Laurie Rogers, Bonnie Bickel, Alyssa Reilly, David Sechrist, Naomi "Mimi" Porter, and our incredible police trainers and tactical operations team headed by Robert (a real man's man)—Flint, Randy, and Rodney. You're helping me change the world one child at a time. You're all awesome!

To the following people and organizations who are an inspiration and are partners in the fight against child trafficking: In Cambodia, my heroes Don and Bridget Brewster and the entire AIM team in Svay Pak, especially Chad Smith (hardest missionary worker I know), Eric Meldrum and the AIM SWAT team (so many rescues!), and Kunthea Meldrum (JOY's liaison in Cambodia); Seng Solida (Lida) and the Precious Women staff; Ginny Hanson of the magnificent Sak Saum; Eric Hanson of In His Steps; special thanks to Dr. Glenn Miles (a tireless worker in the fight); I also have to mention Sam, Chantha, Naret, and the entire staff at the Frangipani Hotel in Phnom Penh, who treat me like family in my Cambodia home away from home; I must also say thank you to Sara, the number-one tuk tuk driver in all Phnom Penh! In India, James Varghese and the Indian Rescue Mission team—Dastigir (Dusty), Viraj, Vikas, and Vaibhav—who have all risked their lives with me in going undercover to see many rescues happen. Across America, Dr. Kalyani Gopal (another co-worker in the fight); my special friend and padawan Gabrielle Thompson of Free for Life International (God has great things in store for you); Nancy Rivard of Airline Ambassadors International; and tireless workers Gwen Adams, Adam Legg, Donna Thompson, and the incredible teams at Priceless and Love Alaska; and Michelle Overstreet of MyHouse.

Mark Edgar for keeping the IRS (and me) happy; and our attorney, Michael Reagor, for keeping JOY legal.

I have to mention Tom McNulty for walking two million barefoot steps; Bill and Lee Medrano for always being there for Gail; Pat and Sandy Olearnick, the epitome of a true Christian couple; Grant and Caroline Stailey and their incredible family; and Jim Rogers, the only man who was with me in Cambodia the day I decided to go barefoot!

Special thanks to Dr. David Linn and the Conifer Medical Center staff and Dr. Roy Thompson and the entire staff at Boulder Heart and Boulder Community Hospital—without you and your teams I would not be alive! Thanks for keeping me going!

To the many flight attendants, gate agents, and 1K phone people at United Airlines: you make me feel so special and truly treat me like royalty as I travel the world in search of the least of these. I don't care what anyone else says—to me you are *the* best airline in the world!

A special acknowledgment to three very special people who passed away too soon this past year: my dear friend Pastor Densel Ball, who continually prayed for and encouraged me; Reverend Ed Mast, my first pastor and the man who introduced me to my Lord and Savior, Yeshua, for believing in me and spending countless hours discipling me; and my brother-in-love Stan Finkelstein, who was the epitome of strength and fortitude in the face of extreme adversity in his fight against cancer.

I could not have an acknowledgments page without recognizing the amazing Alaska Barefoot Mile team put together by Josh Pepperd and his company, Davis Constructors and Engineers, of Anchorage, Alaska. Your marvelous and dedicated team—Jenith Flynn along with Darla, Susan, Sheila, and everyone else who was involved from Davis Constructors—helped bring the Barefoot Mile to a new level. Congratulations on winning the well-deserved national AGC (Associated General Contractors) in the Community Award for 2018.

A very special acknowledgment must also go to my children, Jeni (thanks, Shmergen) and Lance and Meghan (my daughter-in-love), and my wonderful grandchildren, Izac (who now truly knows my heart), Emma, Leah, Malakai, Asher, Izzy, and Gina. Thanks for putting up with me all these years during my times of writing and being away during birthdays and holidays while on rescue missions.

To my incredible ninety-year-old mom, Roz Brodsky, and my wonderful sister, Fran Finkelstein. You two are an inspiration in fortitude, strength, and courage.

Finally, to all the children, teens, and young women who have been rescued and especially those still crying out for their freedom—this book is for you.

The King will say to those on His right hand,
"Come, you blessed of My Father, inherit the kingdom
prepared for you from the foundation of the world:
for I was hungry and you gave Me food;
I was thirsty and you gave Me drink;
I was a stranger and you took Me in;
I was naked and you clothed Me;
I was sick and you visited Me;
I was in prison and you came to Me."

Then the righteous will answer Him, saying,
"Lord, when did we see You hungry and feed You,
or thirsty and give You drink?
When did we see You a stranger and take You in,
or naked and clothe You?
Or when did we see You sick, or in prison, and come to You?"
And the King will answer and say to them,
"Assuredly, I say to you,
inasmuch as you did it to one of the least of these My brethren,
you did it to Me."

MATTHEW 25:34-40

PART 1

THE
SEARCH
FOR
THE
LEAST

INTRODUCTION

In the Red-Light District

Anyone who does anything to help a child is a hero to me.
FRED ROGERS

I turned to Viraj and growled.

"What is this?"

"What do you mean?" my Indian friend almost whispered.

"Do you see *young* girls here?"

I kept my voice low but loud enough so the man who ran the brothel could overhear, firm enough so my displeasure was clear. We were on a mission.

"Do *they* look *young* to you? Do *they* look *twelve* or *thirteen* years old?"

Viraj's head wobbled from side to side. In India—where we were—they call this the head bobble, or Indian headshake. Sometimes the gesture signals a nonverbal "I understand." More often the head bobbler bobs instead of saying no or "I don't know."[1] I wasn't sure with Viraj. He might have been following our script, or he might have become flummoxed. Either way, he knew we had to be convincing.

"Do *any* of these women look *young* to you?" I repeated, raising my voice to a bark. "No! These are *old* women!"

Viraj's eyes bugged, and his head bobbled again, faster this time; he seemed to be embarrassed.

"I hired you to find me *young girls*! *Where are they?*"

Now my voice filled the room, my torso shook, and my right hand tightened its grip on my walking cane.

The brothel owner just stared. His gaze moved from Viraj to me and back to Viraj as if he were watching a ping-pong match.

Five women stood before us. They showed no emotion but glued their eyes to the drama too. Had they been trafficked from Nepal, or were they orphans from nearby Indian slums? Back then I didn't know enough to know the difference. All I knew was that while these women were for sale, they were not the ones I had come to find. They were all at least in their mid-twenties. Too old.

I breathed heavily, sounding a bit like an orc in a *Lord of the Rings* movie. My eyes darted about, and beads of sweat formed a line across my forehead. Was I the craziest visitor ever? Perhaps.

My untucked, oversized Hawaiian shirt, blue jeans, and Rockports screamed "American tourist." No doubt everyone in the room presumed that my pockets bulged with money. Why wouldn't they? Middle-aged, English-speaking travelers don't just stumble upon this hovel of a brothel—a nondescript rundown storefront on a side street surrounded by side street after side street of brothel after brothel in sticky, humid Kamathipura—Mumbai's notorious red-light district. Foreign businessmen come here looking for something very specific. They come to buy girls.

The brothel boss took two steps toward us as if to quiet me. He flicked a Lucky Strike cigarette in his left hand, seeming to silently indicate, "Hurry up. Decide."

Indian men often look younger than they are. Some brothel owners are about the same age as the women in their lineup, but this one seemed older, even middle-aged. He wore a traditional lungi from his waist down and a trendy, long-sleeved casual cotton shirt. A lungi is basically a sarong for men. The shirt might have been a Louis Philippe or Van Heusen. Bright red. No doubt made in India. His attire, like much of his culture, was a patchwork of East meeting West.

Pointing a finger at Viraj, I roared loader, "If they can't bring me *young* girls, we're *leaving*."

Another friend, Dusty, had come with us. Viraj turned to Dusty, desperate for help. Was I going to explode? All Viraj got from Dusty was a halfhearted head bobble that clearly meant "I don't know."

Just as we had rehearsed, Viraj turned and approached the brothel boss. The tension was as thick as the Mumbai air. My friend had to play his part well, or we would lose the moment. He knew why there were no young girls in the lineup. The man in the lungi was being cautious, checking us out. He was trying to figure out whether I was just another American pervert or with the police.

Viraj waved his arms and bobbled his head, faster now. He negotiated hard—at least it looked that way to me—but he was speaking in Hindi, so I didn't understand a word.

My walking cane, which I didn't really need, gave me an appearance of being debonair, but it also served as a means of self-defense, just in case I was attacked. As Viraj pressed the still stone-faced brothel boss, I stood up and rapidly tapped the business end of the cane against the tiled floor. Addressing no one in particular and everyone in the room at the same time, I huffed, "Let's go! I don't have time to waste. I'm a businessman, and I know what I want! C'mon."

Finally the man with the Lucky Strike in his hand nodded. He would bring in more women. I nodded too and sat down.

A faded green and gold curtain separated the room we were in from a narrow hallway that led to who knew where. One by one the original five women disappeared behind the curtain. Just as quickly, five new ones appeared. Another lineup.

I jumped to my feet, almost falling over. These women were just as old as those in the first set.

"What is this!"

This time I actually screamed and used a word I never use.

"Are you f—in' kidding me! Why are you wasting my time?"

Sensing that we were near a breakthrough, I cursed again and pounded my cane. Thump! Thump! Thump! My curly white hair fluttered in every direction, and the beads of sweat on my forehead formed little puddles.

"I'm done with you! You're fired!" I said, pointing at Viraj. "You obviously don't know what *young* means."

Viraj feigned shock—or had his alarm become real?

"Dusty, you are now my guide. Let's go."

I turned and headed toward the exit.

"Wait! Wait!" Viraj pleaded. "They'll bring out more girls. They are young. You'll see."

I took a deep breath and nodded. This time I did not sit down. I just turned slightly and leaned against my cane. I let the doubt in my eyes do the talking.

The parade of women was repeated: five retreated behind the faded curtain, and four new faces emerged.

I relaxed and smiled.

"Yes! Yes! Yes! This is what I've been waiting for."

At least two of the girls were young teens, thirteen or fourteen— just children, really. Sadness stung my heart. My search had taken me many miles and many years. Jesus had told His disciples to care "for the least of these." I had taken Jesus' words to heart many years before—*but who were the least?* Where were they? In that brothel in Mumbai, I thought I might find some of the least. I was close, but I could not let any emotion show. Not yet.

Waiting a beat, I surveyed the girls, making eye contact with each one. Who would I choose? Everyone in the room wanted to know. I hesitated as if I could not decide. Then I turned to Dusty for his opinion. I was buying time.

Dusty breathed deeply and squinted. He was buying time too. Finally, he waggled his head and winked. That was our signal. He had gotten video of the girls with his hidden camera. Our plan was working.

I wanted to cry, but I had to stay on mission.

"These two," I said, pointing to the youngest. "I want them."

I held up fifty dollars—two U.S. twenties and a ten.

"Hold these two girls for me until tomorrow. I am having a party."

The man who ran the brothel nodded and pocketed the money. With another nod he pointed Viraj, Dusty, and me toward the door. We had known this was how it would go, but that didn't make leaving the young girls behind any easier. I wanted to swoop them up and carry them to safety. Instead we smiled and retreated.

We hailed an auto rickshaw and went straight to the local police station. The video Dusty had recorded was sufficient evidence to convince law enforcement to arrange a raid on the brothel. Since 1987, child prostitution has been outlawed in India, so they really had no choice.

The next morning butterflies churned in my stomach as we followed the police to the brothel. Several officers approached the front door and knocked loudly.

Bang! Bang!

No one answered.

Bang! Bang! Bang!

Still no response.

One young officer kicked open the door, and armed troopers swarmed in behind him. I followed.

That's when my stomach dropped—the dank storefront was empty. There was no trace of the owner or the girls. Even the faded curtain was gone. It was as if they had all vanished into thin air.

We lost them!

I wanted to scream. Then I wanted to cry.

The criminals have thwarted us, and those terrified young girls will continue being exploited and abused!

My thoughts swirled in circles. I ached inside.

Only later did we learn that corrupt police officers had tipped off the brothel boss. When we heard the news, I turned to Viraj and Dusty, sighed, and wobbled my head. We had gotten so close to freeing one or two of the least of them—so very close.

1

Tears for Heidi

If you hear someone scream, you shouldn't close the drapes.
You should help. You've got to try.
SHIRLEY TEMPLE BLACK

Call me meshuga, but *Heidi* always makes me cry.

The first time I watched the classic film about the travails of an adorable orphan, I was sprawled barefoot in front of our new black-and-white television set. I was six, maybe seven or eight, years old—I cannot remember for sure. I do know that Heidi was in trouble. Shirley Temple's characters were always in a jam.

Heidi's aunt had snatched her from the mountaintop home she had shared with her grandfather and whisked her away to the big city. *How could her aunt be so cruel?* I sobbed silently. A few scenes later, my curly haired friend was being sold as a domestic worker, really a slave, for another family. I bawled and wanted to rescue her. But in the end, after all kinds of heartache, Heidi was reunited with her grandfather. I think I jumped in the air and cheered.

The movie closed with Heidi saying a prayer: "Please make every little boy and girl in the world as happy as I am. Amen."

That's when my heart for the lowest of the low began. I didn't know it at that point in my life, but decades later Heidi's prayer would become my prayer too. I would discover just how many boys and girls on planet Earth suffer as no child should ever suffer. Just how many are hungry, orphaned, naked, and abused.

Mind you, on that Saturday morning when I was a kid, I was not looking for anything in particular other than some smiles. This was the late 1950s or early '60s, the years NBC broadcast *Shirley Temple's Storybook*. The network also aired her older movies, filmed twenty years or so earlier, when the actress had been a child like me—films like *Heidi*. I devoured them all.

Every time I watched a Shirley Temple movie, from the kitchen my mom could hear my emotional outpouring. She no doubt smiled and scrubbed another dish clean. Years later she told me that my sensitive nature traced back at least in part to these movies about children in dire straits.

I grew up in Brooklyn's East Flatbush district. In the 1950s our neighbors were mostly Italian or Jewish. Some of our Jewish neighbors were Orthodox, others not so much. But the more conservative families at least put on a show of following the Shabbat rules every Friday at sundown. They walked rather than drove to synagogue on Friday night, and they never shopped or did repairs until after sundown Saturday night. The more liberal among us, like the Brodskys, never followed Shabbat rules. Behind closed doors our floors were mopped, and we kids had to clean up our rooms.

Don't get me wrong, we were Jewish enough. We went to synagogue and had bar mitzvahs. We learned about Moses, the great liberator of our people; we honored Yom Kippur (the day of atonement); we celebrated Passover, Rosh Hashanah, and Hanukkah. Passover was my favorite, though I liked receiving gifts at Hanukkah too.

At a Passover seder (or meal), the children always went on a search for the afikomen—a special piece of matzah bread that represented the way the Jewish people had left Egypt. The afikomen was wrapped in a white napkin and hidden. The child who found it got a prize, usually a few coins or some chocolate.

The Brodsky clan had emigrated from Eastern Europe, from Minsk, Russia, and from Poland. We spoke enough Yiddish to know that *meshuga* means crazy. The Brodskys were Jewish—we just didn't follow all the rules. We focused more on living out the American dream. Yes, my mother always wanted me to grow up to become a doctor or lawyer. Some stereotypes are true.

By the late 1950s, the Great Depression was in our rearview mirror, and the Second Great War was settled. America and our allies had won. We heard heinous stories of Hitler's Holocaust and would never forget, but with these tragedies behind us, we had reason to hope for the future. Yes, things were looking up.

As a grade schooler at Public School 159, I learned the three Rs, and Mrs. Harrison taught my classmates and me to think for ourselves. My lessons came easily for me. Perhaps I learned quickly because I was curious about everything. Where did the stars hide during the daylight hours? What made the Ferris wheel at Coney Island spin in circles? How did clowns make people laugh?

As much as I loved school, I relished summers. In those days it was generally safe for us to walk in our neighborhood, though a few infamous gangs had sprung up.

One thing I liked to do was collect pop bottles that grownups had discarded. I could get two cents for the small ones and five cents for the large ones at the local supermarket. On a good day I might earn fifty cents—enough for an admission ticket to the movies.

Another thing I enjoyed was clowns. Clarabell was the first clown I ever saw. He was the star of the *Howdy Doody* television show. Clarabell never spoke a word until his last episode in 1960, when he said, "Goodbye, kids." Of course, I was shocked. How could Clarabell go away? I heard sounds of sobbing from the television set as "Auld Lang Syne" played quietly over the end credits. I was a blubbering mess.

Bozo was on television too. He spoke, laughed, and wore outrageous wigs. Ronald McDonald came along later. He was really just a salesman in a clown outfit and big shoes.

Clarabell and Bozo were funny and brought me joy, but the best clowns were the live ones. My dad often took our whole family to the Ringling Brothers and Barnum & Bailey Circus in Manhattan. By then the two great big-top shows had become one, and it featured lots of clowns.

Blinko and Frankie were silly and sad. Emmett Kelly was their hobo clown. He could make you laugh until your sides split. I wouldn't be surprised if that is where the phrase "side splitting" came from! Without saying a word, Kelly could command an audience. His act was art. He fascinated me.

Secretly I wanted to be a clown.

My father had other, more practical ideas for me. He drove a truck for a living. One route took him across the river and into Manhattan. Sometimes I rode with him. One stop was near the famous Bowery—Manhattan's skid row. There, for the first time, I saw ragged, unshaven, downcast men known as the Bowery boys. They were queued for soup. And they saw me.

I didn't cry, but I was shaken. What I witnessed wasn't what should be. In hindsight, I think this is what my father wanted me to see so that I would remember. Remembering is a big part of our Jewish ethos.

I didn't know it then, but my heart for the least started in my childhood. Or at least some seeds were planted.

Being Jewish meant I didn't know much about Jesus or His words. Of course, I had heard about the Gentiles' God, walked past huge Catholic cathedrals, and learned that my Italian friends prayed to Mary, but I knew no more. I knew nothing of Jesus' call to remember the hungry, the poor, the naked, the oppressed, and, yes, the orphan.

I knew nothing, yet somehow I did know.

2

A Nice Jewish Boy

In a gentle way, you can shake the world.
MAHATMA GANDHI

I t was a run-of-the-mill school day. My sixth-grade teacher had written a list of names on the chalkboard. Each of us was to pick a name, research all the details about that person's life, and write a mini-biography about him or her. I perused the choices: Thomas Edison, Harriet Tubman, Abraham Lincoln, Winston Churchill, Mark Twain, Babe Ruth. I had heard of them all until I came to one: Gandhi.

What a cool name! And what a challenge to dig into the life of someone I had never heard of. Mahatma Gandhi.

Being a research freak, I almost ran to the library and asked to see all the books about this new person in my sixth-grade world. Wow, how my eyes were opened. Gandhi, of course, was an advocate for the poorest of the poor. He gave up his career as an attorney, made his own clothes, and traveled throughout his nation, which I quickly learned was India.

I have always loved quotes, and Gandhi had some of the best and deepest. It was he who said, "You may never know what results come of your actions, but if you do nothing, there will be no results."

Looking back, the character trait in me of wanting to take action had roots in that sixth-grade homework assignment. How cool was it that I got to make multiple trips to India later in life!

But before I get too far ahead of my story, let me give you a little backstory about me.

Becoming a Man

As a nice Jewish boy growing up in Brooklyn, New York, I was bar mitzvahed at the age of thirteen. To this day, more than fifty years later, I can tell you what I had for every meal that day as well as numerous things that occurred from the time I awoke until I went to bed sometime around two thirty in the morning.

That day, November 13, 1965, I woke up before the sun and did some final study for the most significant day of my life up to that point. I was an emotional basket case. I showered and meticulously combed my hair and then sat down to a breakfast of scrambled eggs, home fries, sausages, an English muffin, and orange juice. I dressed carefully in my suit and tie, and then we were off.

At the synagogue, I was shaking. In thirty minutes I would be standing at the front to recite my haftarah—in Hebrew! This was the Scripture portion I had been studying twice a week at Hebrew school for the past two years. Oy vey! I was scared.

Despite being able to remember everything I ate that day, I can barely recall my recitation. I do know I felt pride when I was finished. "Today you are a man," I was told.

Sadly, things from that day on went terribly wrong. The tradition I had experienced was wonderful, the ceremony thrilling, but my preparation for manhood had been only partial. Now that I was supposedly a man, how was I supposed to act? What were the purposes and long-term goals of being a man? I had memorized some passages of Scripture at Hebrew school, but everything I had learned was tradition and had no practical meaning for me.

So I surmised that the only way to be a man was to do what men did. My father smoked, so I took up smoking at the age of thirteen. Nobody taught me what it meant to have excellent character, a good reputation, morality, integrity, honor, or destiny. In the months following my bar mitzvah, I quickly became disillusioned. I was in the temple so infrequently after the age of thirteen that sin became commonplace for me. If I felt the need for forgiveness, I could always go to the temple one day a year on Yom Kippur, say a series of prayers, and come out feeling free—at least until the next cigarette, pipeful of marijuana or hashish, or off-color remark about the opposite sex. By the age of fifteen, I was heavily involved with drugs and drug dealing. My life was a disaster.

When my older brother, Steven, died from cancer at age eighteen, I abandoned my belief in the God of Abraham and all other religions. I found faith of any kind a complete waste of time. I was sixteen. How could the God who called us Jews His chosen people allow someone to suffer the way my brother had? In fact, why hadn't He taken me instead? In addition to my drug use, I was now involved in illicit sex, and I had dropped out of high school. My brother had had everything to live for, and I was making a shambles of my life.

Aware now that my life could be snatched from me at any time, I decided to live it up while I had the chance. For the next two years, I had as much fun as possible. At eighteen I joined the Air Force, where they tried to make a man out of me, but I was stubborn and still determined to get as much fun out of life as I could.

When I got out of the Air Force, I wandered from job to job for several years. It was at one of those jobs, selling cute puppies in a pet store to unwitting customers, where I met Gail. Eight months later, on October 27, 1974, we were married.

Nobody thought our marriage would last—my parents, her parents, my friends, her friends. Even though Gail and I have now been married forty-three years, our family and friends would actually have been pretty right on if one thing had not occurred: we both received Jesus as our Messiah and Lord two years after our marriage.

Yeshua the Messiah

Several months after getting married, Gail and I moved to Fountain Hills, Arizona, because we wanted to raise a family in a place completely different from New York. I became highly involved in the community—I started a business, joined the Kiwanis club, got involved in the local school system.

At a meeting I attended for the elementary school, people were discussing which minister to invite to pray before a special event the school was planning. I became enraged. I pounded my fist on the desk and shouted, "No way! That's against the law. If you bring anybody into this school to pray, you'd better bring the one they're praying to, or I'll sue this school for every penny I can get!" Silence filled the room. The discussion was over.

At the end of the meeting, a woman came over to me. She was the first real Christian who had ever spoken to me. I won't ever forget her words: "I've never met anyone like you. I'm going to pray for you every day until God reveals Himself to you."

"Don't waste your time," I retorted.

I didn't know it until after I received Jesus as my Messiah, but that dear, precious, sweet sister went home and called every prayer chain she could find throughout the United States. God was literally bombarded from that day on with the name "Jeff Brodsky."

In no more than a week, I started to run into Christians everywhere! For the first twenty-four years of my life, I had never seen a real Christian, and now when I went into a restaurant, I heard people right next to me praying over their meals. I couldn't remember seeing that happen a single time in my life. Now I saw evidence of Christians around me almost daily.

The first time I met the man who led me to the Lord was when I went to complain to him about a problem at the Kiwanis club. This man, Ed Mast, was the president of the club—and also a pastor. When he gave me the address for where we were to meet, little did I know that it was for his church office. When I arrived at his church, I thought, *No way. I'm not going in there.* But then I thought, *Why not? There's nothing to be afraid of—I don't believe in God anyway.*

Walking into the sanctuary, I was overtaken by the sense I'd felt years earlier whenever I had entered the synagogue. I knew deep within that this was a place people believed was God's house.

When I sat down with Pastor Ed, I was ready to do battle over the matter at the Kiwanis club. But the battle never materialized. It's hard to fight someone who is full of love. Pastor Ed overcame me with his genuineness, and we ironed out our differences rather quickly.

One hot September morning not long after this meeting, the sun shone brightly into my car as I drove down the Beeline Highway. All of a sudden I felt a presence in the car with me. It was so strong that I literally had to stop driving. I pulled the car over and checked it from top to bottom—the trunk, under the seats, under the hood. The presence was so real that it sent a chill up my spine. I don't know how to describe it other than to say that God surely sent an angel or some form of His presence into my vehicle. From that moment to this day, that presence has never left me.

I became obsessed with wanting to know more about God. Questions flooded my mind—questions I had no answers to. But I knew someone who could help me. I called Pastor Ed. I felt I could speak to him on this topic and share the questions burning within me.

Pastor Ed came to my home, and I was astounded at his wisdom. "What about Jesus?" I asked him. "Is He really the promised Messiah? If so, why have the Jews rejected Him?" Pastor Ed left me with a Bible, although I couldn't accept it as the Word of God at that time.

I met with Pastor Ed again, and this time he asked me to come to a church service on Sunday. When I agreed, I was shocked at myself. *How can I go to a church service?* I thought. Yes, I wanted to know more, but deep within I was still a Jew. The more Christians witnessed to me, actually, the stronger my pride for my Jewish heritage grew as I began to fully understand what being part of God's chosen people was all about. Early on in life I had been told that people from other religions were out to get the Jews. But now that I had been approached by genuine Christians, I saw that wasn't true of everybody. Still, my pride for being a Jew rose up within me, and even though I had told Pastor Ed I would go to church, I called some friends that Sunday morning and asked them to go walking in the mountains instead.

But that morning something changed my life forever. As I walked down a hill with my friends, although the path in front of me was smooth, it was if something (or someone) suddenly tripped me. I rolled down the path, and when I came to a stop, my foot radiated excruciating pain. I couldn't stand up—my friends had to carry me to the car. As they drove me to the emergency room, all I could think was, *If only I had gone to church this morning.*

The following Sunday I went on crutches. I sat in the back row, in the chair closest to the exit. Listening to the sermon, it was as if only the pastor and I were in that room. I felt that he could see inside me as he spoke words that pierced my heart. I left that morning with a peace I'd never had before.

The next week the church announced that the following Sunday night they would be showing a movie called *Time to Run* produced by the Billy Graham Evangelistic Association. As I sat at home that week nursing my partially broken foot, I read several books people had given me about the Jewishness of Jesus. I was amazed to discover that Jesus was actually a Jew. I decided I needed to dig into the Old Testament to find out what it said about the Messiah. I was astounded to read all the prophecies regarding who the coming Messiah would be—and how so many of them had been fulfilled in Jesus. After intense study and deep searching, I concluded that Jesus was who He claimed to be—the Messiah. There was no doubt in my mind.

That Sunday night, October 17, 1976, after the movie, Pastor Ed stood before the congregation and invited people to receive Jesus. It was as if the Holy Spirit lifted me from my chair as I stood to accept that invitation. I went with Pastor Ed into his office and prayed to receive Yeshua[1] as my Messiah, and I left that room a new man.

3

A Clown Is Born

To me there is no picture so beautiful as smiling, bright-eyed,
happy children; no music so sweet as their clear and ringing laughter.

P. T. BARNUM

The first time I was a clown, I was sixteen.

My mother was hosting a Hanukkah party, which was a big deal even for liberal Jewish folks. Our family was a large one, and this year for the festivities my mom wanted to hire a clown to entertain the children. Usually clowns had sloppy makeup and were a bit lame or amateurish, at least when compared to Clarabell or Emmett Kelly.

That gave me an idea.

"Mom," I said, "I want to be the clown."

My mom was always my biggest fan when I was growing up. That's how moms are supposed to be, and my mom played out her role to perfection.

Not skipping a beat, she grabbed a mop from the storage closet, and we dyed it red. Magically, we had a wig! I put it on and looked in the mirror. Raggedy Andy's twin! That was the first time I did anything clown-like.

Another seed planted.

Fun in Faith

Years later, when people started hearing that I was a former drug-fueled Jewish teenager from Brooklyn who had accepted Jesus as Messiah, I was invited to share my testimony all over. I spoke at churches and shared my story.

At first it was a thrill to be in a pulpit. At a few places, people's faces lit up, and some even accepted Jesus themselves. But as time went on, I noticed something about too many pew-sitting Christians.

When I accepted Jesus, I was the most excited human on Earth. I couldn't believe that He was really the Messiah. But when I went to speak at churches, I noticed people looking at their watches, tapping their toes, nodding off. I could tell they were thinking, *When is this meeting going to be over?*

I began to call the watch watchers "prune suckers." These people came to church and sat with their hands folded and smug looks on their faces. Where was their joy? They must have been sucking on prunes!

The way I saw things, when the church service was dismissed shouldn't have mattered. We were there to celebrate Jesus! Wasn't the gospel good news to them? It sure was to me. I felt that people should take off their watches and leave them at the door. If these people knew the same Jesus I knew, then they would *want* to be in church.

As one who jumps into the deep end of the pool when I see a need, I jumped. I started Fun in Faith Ministries, even though I had never been to seminary or trained as a lay leader. I knew Jesus, and the prune suckers needed Him too!

My upstart outreach was flush with dreams and hope, and it failed miserably. I didn't know what I was doing. Thankfully,

Pastor Ed was discipling me. I found out that there is a lot one should know before starting in ministry.

Fun in Faith Ministries didn't last long, but I still knew people needed to have fun in their faith.

One week my pastor asked if I could present an object lesson to go along with his Sunday morning message. He was going to talk about the Father, Son, and Holy Spirit and how the Godhead is three in one. I jumped at the offer, but this time I carefully waded into the pool instead of diving into the deep end.

That's when I looked at the idea of the clown character. *Maybe I can do this as a clown*, I thought.

I collected three big boxes and wrapped them in brown paper. On each box I wrote one name: "Father" on the first, "Son" on the second, and "Holy Spirit" on the third.

On Sunday morning I carried the boxes onto the platform. The crowd wasn't looking at their watches now—all eyes were on me. I didn't speak a word but just began to stack the boxes. As I moved them up and down, left and right, I was careful to hide the words I had written on them.

Finally I had the boxes stacked in the right order, revealing the names of the Father, Son, and Holy Spirit. But what did it mean? I stroked my chin as if I were trying to solve a puzzle. With a quick motion, my face lit up, and I pointed at my head and raised my eyebrows happily to indicate that the light had come on. I lifted up the bottom box with the other two stacked on top of it, and I turned the stack around. On the backs of all three boxes, I had written a giant numeral one to illustrate the main point of the message: the Father, Son, and Holy Spirit are a trinity (three), but They are one.

It was my first time in church as a clown.

On the Streets of Berkeley

Over the next year or so, I began to use the clown character to share the gospel. I actually quit my job and started clown ministry full time. You should have seen my first costumes and makeup jobs. They were pathetic. I needed help.

In the late 1970s I found that help at a clown conference at the University of California Berkeley. Avner Eisenberg was one of the featured performers. Also known as Avner the Eccentric for his show of the same name, this man was an incredible vaudeville performer, clown, mime, and juggler. He would later become known for his role in the 1985 movie *The Jewel of the Nile* starring Michael Douglas and Kathleen Turner, in which he played the jewel.

Avner had a totally different style from any of the other clowns. To this day I remember his show. This man had mastered his craft. He could have two thousand people in the palm of his hand, doing whatever he wanted them to do—without saying a word. *I want to do that*, I thought. *I want to command an audience without saying a word. Just by actions.* Avner overwhelmed me.

Besides his ability to mesmerize a crowd, Avner was hilarious. I laughed so hard at his antics that my face hurt. Avner gave me a new understanding of what it meant to laugh.

Several other clowns heavily influenced me during the conference. Bill Peckham was a master clown who was also a United Methodist minister known for his ministry of "Holy Fools." Floyd Shaffer was a pastor too, a Lutheran. Both men preached full services in clown costume without saying a word. Leo "Tug" Remington was there too, and he said something to me that made a deep impact on my soul: "Even children who are starving to death deserve the dignity of laughter." Another famous person would make that exact statement to me a year or so later, further confirming an aspect of God's call on my life to minister His joy to those who are at their very lowest.

I was already a clown, but I didn't know what I was doing. I had been playing it by ear. But when I saw Avner and these other great clowns, I knew I could up my game.

I told Bill Peckham, Floyd Shaffer, and Leo Remington what I had being doing, and they helped me brainstorm my clown character. What was my personality? What clowning style did I like—hobo, Auguste, circus? Who did I want to become? These guys helped me come up with amazing makeup—large white circles around my eyes and another around my mouth, with black outlines surrounding them, creating a cheerful heart-shaped expression. Topped off with a red clown nose and my new interstellar propeller beanie hat, I looked like the real deal. Not only that, but I reflected the little boy I wanted to be—a happy child who could innocently and unaffectedly reach out to hurting people. When that white makeup went on, it was symbolic to me—Jeff Brodsky had died, and Snuggles the Clown had come to life. It was a picture of being born again.

The night the conference ended, I wanted to try out what I had learned and test out my new clown character, so I did what in the clown world we call "taking the plunge"—I hit the streets of Berkeley as Snuggles the Clown. I put on my new makeup and red clown nose and donned a makeshift costume—rolled-up jeans, a colorful shirt, my interstellar propeller beanie. I had seen people living on the streets, and I wanted to see if I could make them laugh.

I walked from campus toward what looked like a main street, interacting with people along the way. I waved and nodded at people, and everyone I engaged smiled or laughed. Snuggles seemed to be working!

It was late, but I was having so much fun. I thought about heading back to the campus, when I noticed a guy leaning against a post, apparently sound asleep. Actually, he was high as a kite. I stopped in front of him and looked into his face, making expressions and trying to wake him up. Suddenly he was startled awake by the red-nosed clown standing in front of him.

The sleeping man jumped. "You're a clown, man!"

I nodded. *Yeah.*

"You're a real clown!"

I nodded very big nods.

"What are you doing here?"

I shrugged my shoulders.

He and I communicated without me saying one word. I realized in that moment that when you don't speak, you are in control. If as a clown I spoke words, it would put the other person in control.

That conference sent me on my journey to make people smile—especially the poorest of the poor. The Bible says that "a merry heart does good, like medicine" (Proverbs 17:22). I wanted to be a doctor of smiles. I would tell people that I was a PhD—a purveyor of happy days.

When I returned home, I collected various pieces to create Snuggles's complete outfit and express his personality, and I taught myself close-up magic tricks that I could use to perform for children.[1] I also started teaching clown classes. When I took my students to homes for seniors, we made sure that from the moment we got into costume until we were finished interacting with people, we didn't speak a word. It was incredible how the clowns brought so much joy and life to people.

Snuggles for the Hungry

When I became Food for the Hungry International's ambassador to children in Third World countries in 1979, I quickly thought of using Snuggles. Few missionaries wear a red clown nose and big, pointy shoes. But the clown character I had created, which affectionately became known around the world as Snuggles the Love Clown, was an excellent tool for grabbing the attention of children and making them smile.

Snuggles was what's called the Auguste style of clowns, known for their clumsiness. They're real rabble rousers! I loved his classic big red clown nose, the propeller on his zany, multi-colored hat, and his colorful mismatched socks, one with orange and white horizontal stripes, the other with a ridiculous blue and white stripe.

In true Auguste fashion, his huge rainbow-striped suspenders held up his baggy checked trousers, which sported large pockets for his magic tricks, juggling balls, scarves, and small giveaway treats. Most noticeable were his mouth and eyes covered in a heart-shaped mask of white face paint surrounded by a thick black border and, of course, how he clomped around in his huge yellow and red shoes.

Snuggles went on my first overseas trip with Food for the Hungry. We went to Thailand, Bangladesh, and India—where my eyes were opened to a new world of abject poverty. It's one thing to know that severe poverty exists. It's another to see it up close. Anyone who has ever gone on a missions trip understands. Before embarking upon the trip, the person learns about the place they'll serve and the people who live there. But not until a person actually looks into the faces of people and hears their stories do they truly get it. When I started traveling overseas, poverty came into clear focus for me.

Not only did I see the hungry and naked, but I also awakened to a world of injustice and prejudice, especially when I visited the Vietnamese refugees (known historically as the Vietnamese boat people). These beautiful folks had escaped their war-torn nation only to find themselves living in horrid refugee-camp conditions in Thailand, Singapore, and Malaysia. Literally thousands of people were crammed together like sardines into makeshift villages. With tens of thousands of refugees escaping, local governments, the United Nations, and humanitarian organizations couldn't keep up with the demand for basic needs such as food, water, housing, and medical care.

As Snuggles, I reached out to the destitute. Wherever I walked, huge crowds of people followed. The children, especially, loved Snuggles. After all, it wasn't every day that a colorful clown from America roamed through the refugee camps. In full character I galumphed up and down the narrow paths lined with thousands of crude shelters constructed from boat timbers, plastic sheeting, flattened tin cans, and palm fronds.

As I juggled and did my magic tricks, delivering a message of hope in Christ, I did what I could to bring a little joy into the lives of these people who simply wanted to have a country to call their own. I focused specifically on the thousands of children, trying to bring smiles to their faces with my juggling, magic tricks, and, of course, hilarious pratfalls.

Each time I put on the clown makeup and affixed the hat, nose, and colorful clothes, I was transformed into a different person with big clown pockets stuffed full of surprises. Everywhere I went, I became a fifteen-minute phenomenon with my routine that I called the Snuggles pocket circus. I could be on a street in India or in a village in Uganda—it did not matter. All it took was making colored scarves appear seemingly from thin air, and soon I was surrounded by dozens of people.

Within minutes of being in the hundred-degree heat and suffocating humidity, even before I began walking and stopping along my route to perform yet another routine, I was soaked with sweat. The refugee families didn't see a clown but rather an artist.

Snuggles was not like a goofy Bozo the Clown or the hamburger salesman Ronald McDonald. Part of Snuggles's effect was never speaking. God showed me an inspired way to present the gospel during those performances—the whole story of Jesus, including His birth, death, and resurrection—without saying one word. I took a cue from Floyd "Socataco" Shaffer, a master clown and Lutheran minister and one of the men who had helped me at the clown conference. In the early 1970s, Shaffer became famously known for donning a clown suit and makeup each Sunday to reach his congregation through mime. He told the *Weekly World News,* "Humor is a gift of God. . . . I decided to conduct my own wordless services using the childlike, gentle clown to give God's message a different form."[2]

I restructured Floyd's effective routine to fit the character of Snuggles and, like Shaffer did, I saw multitudes of people accept Jesus into their lives. As Snuggles, I spoke only with my body, actions, and emotions. But once my routine was over, I had earned the right to be heard. Then, taking another cue from Shaffer,

I removed my makeup and talked to the gathered people, young and old alike. Like Shaffer discovered, the key was knowing who I was talking to and then presenting the gospel in ways that resonated with that audience. With both children and adults, Snuggles shared the gospel in the simplest, most childlike way.

I've long admired Mother Teresa, also known as the Saint of the Gutters. She led a powerful, globally known ministry yet was a very simple person. She (along with the Sisters of Charity) spent their days walking the slums of Calcutta and bringing the dying to Nirmal Hriday (Place of the Immaculate Heart), the home for the destitute she had opened in 1952. There, the nuns bathed and fed the dying and placed them on cots. Anyone who knows anything about this woman of God realizes that Mother Teresa believed everyone should have the opportunity to die with dignity.

As Snuggles, I visited Nirmal Hriday and brought smiles to the poorest of the poor in Calcutta. Mother Teresa personally invited me. In her note asking me to come and minister, she wrote, "Even those who are dying of starvation deserve the dignity of laughter." Wow. The exact words Leo Remington had spoken to me at the clown conference.

These words have never left me.

4

The Love Clown

*Love is that condition in which
the happiness of another person is essential to your own.*
ROBERT A. HEINLEIN

At a Vietnamese refugee camp in Ubon on my first trip to Thailand, Snuggles's name was officially expanded. Until then, I had just been Snuggles. Now I became Snuggles the Love Clown.

The late Dr. Hal Stack was a pastor and Food for the Hungry relief worker. As a young man, he had played a year of professional baseball in the Pittsburgh Pirates minor-league system. It was Dr. Stack who led our group to the refugee camp. His job was to guide me and make sure I arrived on time to the places I was supposed to visit.

One day Dr. Stack told me about a Vietnamese refugee who had walked over to watch me entertain the children. In broken English the old man had asked him, "Who dis guy?"

"He's Snuggles—a clown from America."

"What he do here?"

"He wants to make people happy—to make the children laugh."

"Why he do dis?"

"Because he loves everybody."

"Ohhhh, so dis guy Snuggles da Ruv Crown?"

"Yes, that's right," Dr. Stack laughed. "He's Snuggles the Love Clown!"

When Dr. Stack told me that story, my heart laughed with joy. From that day on, he always introduced me as Snuggles the Love Clown, and the heartfelt term of endearment stuck.

God can and will use our obedience to His call on our lives to touch people in need through the gifts and talents He has given to us. In Paul's first letter to the Corinthians, he tells us that we are "fools for Christ's sake" (1 Corinthians 4:10). I took that scripture literally. In taking on the character of a fool for Christ, I actually became a tool that Christ could use to touch others.

The Least of These?

During my years of traveling and performing as Snuggles the Love Clown, several times I thought I had found the lowest of the low, or what Jesus calls "the least of these" in Matthew 25:45. One time was when I met the Telugu people in Bangladesh. These people live in such abject poverty that most Westerners can't fathom it. Because they are ethnically Indian and Hindu, they are *dalit*s, or outcasts, in this Muslim nation.

Soon after I arrived in Bangladesh, I was walking as Snuggles on a mud road in a village where the huts were literally constructed of garbage. As I trundled along, my giant red and yellow leather clown shoes flopped with each step. At one point my host pointed to a small hut fashioned out of cardboard and plastic and said, "Mr. Snuggles, a Christian family lives there."

I went up close to the hut, which sat right next to the city garbage dump. It had been made out of whatever suitable garbage the family had been able to find—anything to partially keep out the elements. It's fairly common in the Third World for people in poverty to live in or next to a dump. The dump becomes somewhat of a survival source for them, as they scavenge for "building" items to sell and even food. The dwellings of the Telugu of Bangladesh had dirt floors. In front of the house I stood near was a tiny canal, only a few inches wide—this was the family's bathroom. An endless stench of rotting food and human and animal waste penetrated the air.

A young emaciated woman stood outside the hut. I thought I would just do my clown thing and make this family smile. But God had a bigger idea. The young woman greeted us by putting her hands together in the traditional position in front of her face, almost as if she were praying. Her dark hair was rolled tightly into a bun, a stick holding it in place. My host chatted with her, and then her husband stepped out. He smiled and greeted us, visibly excited. He invited us into their home.

The only piece of furniture on the dirt floor inside was an old handmade bamboo bench. On one of the rickety plastic walls hung a tattered copy of a painting of Jesus by Warner Sallman—the "Head of Christ" portrait that hangs in millions of homes around the world. That was it. No beds, no table, just an eight-by-eight-foot room of almost nothing. *Oh my*, I thought. *You can't get any lower than this.*

The husband insisted that I sit on the bamboo bench, while the wife called for all the children to come. My heart melted as I realized I didn't need to do a thing; all seven children already had huge smiles on their faces. When they saw me, they were almost beside themselves to see this colorful American clown in their home.

The seven children knelt before me, putting their hands together in front of their faces. They bowed, touching their heads to the ground (the highest form of greeting and respect shown to a guest). Just as quickly as they had knelt, they rose to their feet and began singing in English, "Mine eyes have seen the glory of the coming of the Lord."

When their small but exuberant voices sang, "Glory, glory, Hallelujah," the lump in my throat and the tears in my eyes gave me away. No longer was I a jolly character ready to entertain and amuse children. Instead I was simply a man in clown makeup filled with humility and joy.

As this unexpected choir sang, a bright white haze began to fill the room, as if a halo had surrounded us. It was as if I was in a glorious dream. When the children finished their song, they knelt and bowed again. After my tearful applause, I managed to perform some goofy Snuggles antics. Their wide smiles somehow got even wider. I felt the purest sense of joy in that little hut.

The mother came forward and knelt before me. She examined my huge, mud-covered clown shoes like a Jewish mother would have done. Instead of shaking a finger at me, she merely gently removed the wooden stick that held her long hair back. She bowed before me and began to wipe the mud off my shoes with her long, dark tresses. If I hadn't already been a speechless clown, I would have been utterly speechless. As it was, I was humbled beyond any humility I had previously known.

What a selfless and beautiful act! Overwhelming. I was a flood of emotions that took over all my senses. I was completely undone, weeping uncontrollably. The memory still brings tears.

I immediately took hold of this woman's shoulders, lifted her up, and tenderly tried to stop her. She looked at me, smiling radiantly, and as I looked into her eyes, tears streaming down my face, I realized that before me was not a poor Telugu woman from the slums of Bangladesh. She was my *sister in Christ*. I was supposed to be the missionary for the gospel, yet she was the Lord's true servant to me that day.

I have come to realize that God commands us to care for the poor and be voices for the voiceless because, first, it honors Him, and second, our obedience brings us closer to God's heart.

I thought I had gone overseas to share the love of God, but this woman showed me how to share God's love in a completely different way than I had known with the only thing she had: her humility. She saw my need, and the only thing she could think of to meet that need was her hair. That day I gained a deeper understanding of Galatians 3:28 in which Paul says that we are "one in Christ Jesus." *One day,* I thought, *this precious woman from clear across the world and I could be living as neighbors in mansions built by God, walking on streets of gold. Perhaps we will even sit across from each other at the marriage supper of the Lamb.*

I was sure I had found the least of these in the Telugu, but little did I know I would someday discover people far more destitute. Yes, the Telugu undoubtedly needed financial help, but they were also some of the wealthiest people I had ever met. The hand of God rested on that family. Those seven children had no idea how poor they were; instead, their eyes shone with the glory of the coming of the Lord. That day God showed me that the poor will always be with us and that I didn't have to change the way they live, because compared to eternity, our time on Earth is so short. More importantly, God showed me that we should change *who* people are living for. One day this earth will pass away, and for the rest of eternity all God's children will live in paradise—together.

Shaken

My encounter with this godly Telugu family left me an emotional wreck. My host wanted me to go back to the hotel to rest, but I told him I would like to visit a children's hospital instead. After experiencing how others lived in such dire poverty, the last thing I wanted to do was to go to my comfortable hotel. I needed to see children in need and bring smiles to their faces.

My host relented and took me to the Shishu Children's Hospital in Dhaka, the capital city of Bangladesh. I had my Snuggles pocket circus ready—magic tricks, juggling balls, scarves—all the tricks of my trade. I was ready to make some children laugh, so I decided to see every child in that hospital.

Working my way down from the top floor, I visited every child on each of the three floors, accompanied by the hospital administrator, Dr. Akbar. To that point I had fulfilled my goal of making every child smile. We were ready to leave when I heard a child's mournful wail from a secluded room. When I went to see who was crying, Dr. Akbar grabbed my shoulder.

"Where are you going?" he asked.

"There's a child in there crying," I said. "I haven't seen this child yet."

I turned back toward the room, but Dr. Akbar tried to stop me. "Mr. Snuggles, there is nothing you can do for this child." He turned to go, expecting me to follow him. But I went the other way. There was no way I was not going to enter that room.

As I went in, I saw a single bed with a child about seven years old lying on it. A man who was probably his father sat next to the boy holding his trembling hand as the boy shook and cried. When the father saw me, he was clearly bewildered. I'm pretty sure not too many colorful clowns with big red noses from America had visited that place. I motioned to the father with my hands as if to say, "No worries. I'm the American clown. I'll stop the child from crying." *After all*, I thought to myself, *I've never met a child yet whom I couldn't make smile.*

I did everything I could to bring a smile to that little boy's face. I performed my entire pocket circus, I did pratfalls, I even rubbed my big red nose on his. Nothing worked. After a long time, exhausted from the emotion, I lifted the old gray blanket covering the little boy, and what I saw shook me to my core. The child was completely emaciated, starving to death. For the second time that day, my thoughts expressed my heartbreak: *Oh my. You can't get any lower than this.*

In spite of my very best efforts, I had failed to bring happiness to this boy. To this day, he is one of the only children I haven't been able to make smile. That time instead the clown cried.

That night I barely slept. On my flight home the next day, I couldn't stop thinking, *Why, Lord? Why have You allowed me to witness these terrible things—such extreme poverty, disease, heartache?* And I thought about how every time I believed I had found someone I could describe as the least of these, I discovered a new group, more destitute than those I'd seen before. As anguished questions swirled through my mind, I heard the Lord's quiet answer: *Because I knew you would find a way to do something about them.*

Lepers Need Love Too

Not long after my trip to Bangladesh, I traveled to India, where I visited a colony of leprosy-affected people. The people in the colony in Jamshedpur, India, were all beggars. They had to be, because nobody ever thought about giving a job to someone afflicted with leprosy. I had no idea that this group of almost two hundred people would become one of my greatest (and favorite) audiences.

As Snuggles, I poured out every ounce of available strength in the sweltering heat to entertain and minister to them. Yet their huge smiles and laughter and their applause with stumps that were leprous hands made me believe that perhaps here I had found the lowest of the low. How could life be any worse for people than to have their bodies wasting away before their eyes and to be shunned and discarded by the rest of society?

I visited children's hospitals where many patients were infected with AIDS. I saw children dying of cancer and various terrible diseases. I visited many prisons in my constant search for the least of these. Each time I met a group more destitute, I would think for a moment that surely these people were the least of these.

I knew that Jesus had told us to minister to the least of these— the hungry, the thirsty, the stranger, the naked, the sick, those who were in prison. But was there a particular group at the very bottom that Jesus wanted me to minister to? I didn't know, but I did know that I would do everything in my power to bring His joy to every hurting, broken child I could.

5

Rich Kid, Poor Kid

Jesus loves the little children, all the children of the world.
CLARENCE HERBERT WOOLSTON

In 1979, during my first visit to Bangladesh as Food for the
Hungry's ambassador, I was invited to do a ten-minute television interview as Snuggles the Love Clown at the International
Press Club. In fact, it was the day after I had visited every child in
the Shishu Children's Hospital in Dhaka, where, despite my best
efforts, I had been unable to bring a smile to the face of that starving, emaciated boy.

Expecting a regular press corps, I was surprised to find not only
radio, TV, and newspaper journalists there but also their families.
Everyone had been invited to see Snuggles, the silent clown from
America. I planned to perform my usual Snuggles pocket circus,
thinking I had sufficient material for the ten-minute slot. It was
going to be a piece of cake.

I arrived at the International Press Club with Dr. Hal Stack. The
room was already nearly full of people, including many children

dressed in beautiful outfits. The boys sported formal attire, bordering on suits and ties; the girls wore fancy evening dresses—the kind usually found on older women.

As I had walked from the car to the building, a group of street children had noticed my colorful clown suit. Once I went inside, these children immediately clustered around the windows of the building outside, which were low to the ground, allowing them to see inside. They excitedly jostled for space, desperate to catch a glimpse of Snuggles the Clown with his huge checkered pants, suspenders, and big red nose. Of course, I was intrigued by them too, knowing how much they would enjoy the show.

Inside, the director quickly informed me of a change to the schedule. He asked if I would be willing to take the whole show—a thirty-minute act that would be televised live. *Wow,* I thought. *I'm not at all prepared for a thirty-minute performance.* My oversized Snuggles pockets contained only enough items for a ten-minute show, which I could possibly stretch to fifteen minutes at best. *What would I do for the remaining fifteen minutes?* Feeling a little nervous, I went to Dr. Stack and told him they had extended my segment.

"I haven't come prepared for a half-hour performance," I explained to him, hoping for sage advice. That is exactly what I received, but it left me feeling just as nervous.

"Jeff, I've seen you! I was with you in Thailand, watching you perform for the Vietnamese boat people. You worked for hours. You're a professional, Jeff!" the good doctor encouraged me. "You're a master clown, as far as I'm concerned. I know you can do this."

"Well, okay," I grumbled. "Thanks for the accolades, but I'm still the one who has to come up with everything."

Bring in the Street Urchins!

I stood there for a moment, thinking things through. *What can I do?* Then it struck me. *I need to have those street children come inside.* I went to the director and said, "Those children out there, peeking inside through the windows, I'd like to have them come into the room."

"Oh no, sir!" he exclaimed emphatically. "No! We have a system here, and we cannot allow this. They can watch from outside, but no, we cannot bring them in here with the other children."

"Then I'll have to sit outside with these children," I reasoned, trying to be diplomatic.

"We *cannot* do this!" he said, determined to win.

"Well," I said, shrugging my shoulders, "if this cannot be done, then I won't be able to do my show!"

I don't like giving ultimatums, but sometimes you have to negotiate those things in life you believe are important.

"Wait a minute," he sighed.

The director went over to chat with some bigwig, as far as I could guess, and I watched as they haggled over my unorthodox request.

Finally the big Kahuna nodded his head. "Okay, okay, fine."

So this group of about twelve poor kids was ushered in from outside and seated across the aisle from the wealthy kids—rich and poor together, separated by only a few feet of fresh air. At that time the caste system in Bangladesh was much the same as the rest of South Asia. Higher castes mixing with the scheduled caste[1] (formerly known as *dalits*, or "untouchables") was unheard of, a very real taboo. Allowing a ragged group of street urchins into the room was a big deal. Rigid barriers had been set aside. How I ended my performance was an even bigger deal.

God Loves Everyone

I started out with my standard Snuggles pocket circus routine. After that I pulled one of the long, colorful laces from my clown shoes and hung it around my neck. Then I pulled out a big, stretchy balloon. I showed it to my audience and then, facing the camera, began blowing as hard as I could into the balloon. But it simply wouldn't fill with air (I was purposefully keeping it empty, of course). I kept pretending to try to blow up the balloon.

Throwing my hands up in despair, I faced my audience and then, looking directly into the camera, started gesturing, encouraging everyone to blow toward me. My audience understood that I needed their help to fill the balloon. I motioned for everybody to start blowing big breaths of air toward me. Filling their lungs with air and puffing out their cheeks, they blew air right at me and my empty balloon. Looking triumphant, I turned my head, angling it to catch everybody's air as I mimed sucking their breath inside me. Showing how grateful I was to have all this help, I started filling the balloon with the air they had supposedly blown toward me and repeated the process.

It's working, I mimed to the audience enthusiastically, and I motioned to them to blow more air at me.

They were getting the picture as they saw their air going into me and then into the balloon. The poor kids, the rich kids, my adult audience—all blew air to me. I even imagined all the people at home watching the show on TV blowing air toward me. And all the while, I sucked in this air to put it into the balloon until it was nice and big. I tied the opening of the balloon into a knot without allowing my audience to see the words on the front side of the balloon. They could only see the back of it. Once I had tied the knot, I turned it around to display the message on the front in big capital letters: LOVE.

I then began to demonstrate my "I LOVE you" routine to my audience.

I showed how I loved them all by pointing first to my eye ("I"), then to the word on the balloon ("LOVE"), and finally to everyone in the audience ("you"). I also pointed to the camera to include all the viewers at home. I repeated this scenario but reversed it to express the "you LOVE me" routine, showing how they all loved me.

Then I delivered the kicker: I walked over to one of the children in the wealthy group and, pointing to the child, expressed "I LOVE you." Then I immediately walked over to where the poor children were sitting and expressed the same "I LOVE you" to a child in that group.

Warming to my point, I pointed up to the sky and used the balloon to demonstrate that "God LOVEs us." Then I made it more personal, motioning to my audience that "God LOVEs me" and "God LOVEs you." To demonstrate this more effectively, I pointed at a specific rich child to show that God loved him; then I pointed to a specific poor child to show that God loved him too.

My finale was certainly Holy Spirit-inspired, because up until that point, I hadn't really thought about doing any of what happened next. I took the hand of a rich boy and the hand of a poor girl and had them face each other. They stood there, about two feet apart. I took the shoelace from around my neck and gave one end to the rich boy dressed up in a suit and tie and the other end to the poor girl in rags. I placed the balloon on top of the string they held, and they immediately understood that they had to keep it balanced on the string. While they stood there, working together to keep the balloon balanced, I waved my hands across the crowd, gesturing that "God LOVEs everybody." Finally I turned back to the children with the string, took the balloon, and handed it to the poor girl. Then I walked off the stage. It was exactly thirty minutes!

The audience went wild. Dr. Stack was bawling his eyes out. I was too. I was in that country and in that TV studio for the poor. If it had been up to me, I would have put on a show for those poor children and let the rich kids peek in through the windows—peering from the inside out.

"I've never seen anything like that!" Dr. Stack said. "You are truly a master at your craft."

That was a high compliment. Every clown wants to be considered a master clown.

In the West it's tempting to believe that these stark divisions between rich and poor are not as severe in our culture, but I'm reminded of a passage in Revelation: "You say, 'I am rich, have become wealthy, and have need of nothing'—and do not know that you are wretched, miserable, poor, blind, and naked" (3:17).

It's easy for us to hold on to these social stratifications. But the truth is that no one is exempt from the problems dividing rich and poor.

6

Bring on the JOY

Without a purpose, life is motion without meaning,
activity without directions, and events without reason.
RICK WARREN

When it comes to Scripture, I consider myself a literalist. You probably know the adage: "God said it, I believe it, that settles it." I like that phrase, but I do think it carries some irrelevant information. Actually, I would take out the "I believe it" part. If God said it, that settles it, whether anyone believes it or not.

That is probably why Jesus' words about "the least of these" in the Gospel of Matthew greatly impacted me. These red letters, combined with a Holy Spirit heart compulsion, had set me on a long journey to minister to the least of these and pour my life out for them.

In 1981, after almost two years as an ambassador for Food for the Hungry International, I made the decision to leave FHI and start my own ministry. My tenure with Food for the Hungry stretches back to more than thirty-five-plus years ago, and I will always be grateful to them for that special time. This organization is still working faithfully throughout the world today. They opened my eyes to the great needs of others—knowledge that has changed the trajectory of my life.

Sitting in the back of my friend's car as he drove me home for the last time from Food for the Hungry's headquarters in Scottsdale, Arizona, I thumbed through a Bible in my lap. Have you ever felt as if Jesus gave you a verse for a specific time in your life? Maybe when you were struggling with an important decision or on the cusp of belief in Him. I've talked to countless people who can point to a verse that literally changed their lives. That day was no different for me. As I skimmed through the pages, I came across a verse in John's Gospel that, like the verses in Matthew 25, would change my life and ministry forever: "These things I have spoken to you, that My joy may remain in you, and that your joy may be full" (John 15:11).

The red letters jumped out at me. I read the verse over and over again.

As a professional clown, it was my job to bring joy into people's lives, to make them forget whatever pain, trouble, or sorrow they were going through, even if only for a few minutes. It's like the songwriter who pens words and puts them to music, hoping that the song will take the listener to another place. Make someone laugh (or even smile), and you create instant trust. A new friendship. A unique camaraderie.

As someone who followed Jesus, I truly desired my joy to be "full" and complete, just as Jesus said it would be in John 15:11. If I lived my life by putting Jesus first, others second, and myself last, this would be the best way to experience true JOY: Jesus, others, and you. I decided to use JOY International as the name of my new ministry—with each letter always in uppercase.

Think about all the things we do that bring us joy: listening to music, reading a good book, eating a good meal, playing a sport or a musical instrument, holding the hand of someone you love. But the joy these things bring us is temporary. It's only there *while* we're experiencing these things. When the moment is over, it simply becomes a memory. The only joy that truly lasts forever is the eternal joy of having Jesus' presence in our lives. His presence—with a real understanding of what He did for us, along with the gift of eternal life He gave us—brings us true, complete joy.

As I read this verse, I felt compelled to share this joy with the world. That's how the ministry of JOY International was born. To this day, I still find that putting Jesus first, others second, and myself third creates scenarios in my own life that bring me great joy.

I thought I knew how desperately the world needed the joy I had. I was so wrong. As the Lord led me from one destitute group to another more destitute, my heart broke a little more. The time would come when He would show me a group of people who, to me, fully embodied the least of these, but until then, I would embark on the heart-wrenching yet joy-filled roller-coaster ride God was about to take me on. Only when my heart was completely broken would I be ready to accept and undertake His lifelong calling.

Cross-Country Clown

With JOY International, I continued traveling the world, ministering as Snuggles the Love Clown to anyone who was oppressed or hurting. I constantly looked for new ways to do this and was always inviting others to join me in the work.

Two years into my adventure with JOY International, I came up with what I thought was a fantastic idea: I would ride a bicycle, dressed as Snuggles, across America from Disneyland in California to the United Nations complex in New York City to raise money for orphaned and abandoned children in India. The funds would help build a home for these children. Pedaling more than 3,500 miles across the country as a clown would surely raise not only funds but awareness for our work.

Many people thought I had lost my mind. And they did have good reason to raise their eyebrows. When I made the decision to embark on this journey, I didn't even own a bicycle. When they heard I had never ridden a bicycle more than a few miles and hadn't trained at all, members of the local bicycle clubs said it would be impossible for me to ride from California to New York, at least not without months and months of proper preparation. What they failed to grasp is that I had a greater purpose than their club members could visualize. They couldn't see that the children would be my motivation and the Lord would be my strength. Of this I was certain!

On the first day, I rode seventy-two miles. Lying in bed that night, I wept tears of pain and fear, wondering if my critics had been right. Then I remembered why I was doing it—to raise funds for children in India who were in desperate need. That was all it took each day as I stepped on the bicycle pedal: those needy children—and my Lord. As I recited Scripture and sang praises, I literally gained strength:

The LORD is my strength and song. (Psalm 118:14)

Behold, God is my salvation, I will trust and not be afraid; for the LORD GOD is my strength and song. (Isaiah 12:2, NASB)

I sang along with cassette tapes played on my Walkman, gaining inspiration as I pedaled. One tape was Don Francisco's *The Traveler*; another was John-Michael Talbot's *The Painter*. I also had a few praise and worship records from the Maranatha Singers. While riding across the country, I traversed hills and valleys and climbed many mountains. When pedaling up a mountain, a person's only goal is to reach the top. Time and again, I would finally crest a summit, only to see another hill ahead, followed by another mountain. There was always another obstacle to overcome. The end of my journey was far off, but each peak brought me closer to my goal.

I finally made it across America, reaching New York City in fifty-five days. I was thrilled to find Gail and our two children, Jeni and Lance, there to meet me. Republic Airlines had heard about my ride across the country to raise funds for children in need and had flown my family out as a surprise for me.

But the results of the trip held several disappointments for me. I had intended to go inside the UN building to deliver a message about my ministry to the destitute, but no matter how I explained, they wouldn't let this red-nosed bicycling clown inside. Not only that, but I hadn't raised as much money as I'd hoped to. After riding 3,500 miles in a clown suit across the entire United States, that was a bit of a let down.

For the time being, I was just relieved it was over. I was exhausted—but I wasn't down and out. God would show me how to reach the people He had called me to help.

101 Miles Across Death Valley

Some thirteen years into my work with JOY International, I was reading my Bible one day and came across Psalm 23:4: "Yea, though I walk through the valley of the shadow of death, I will fear no evil; for You are with me." *Hmm*, I thought. *The shadow of death.* As I ruminated on the valley of the shadow of death and how God meant us to be unafraid in that place, the words reminded me of Death Valley.

That brought another thought. *I wonder if I could bring life to Death Valley.*

How could I do that? I had no idea.

But I could research. Since these were the days before the Internet, I headed to the library to find out what I could. What I discovered was interesting. Death Valley National Park in eastern California was part of the Mojave Desert. It was one of the hottest places in the world and also boasted the lowest elevation in North America, in Badwater Basin, at 282 feet below sea level. One of the lowest places in the world, the lowest people in the world—was there a correlation? I wondered if I could do a fundraising walk through Death Valley. I researched temperatures and seasons to see if a walk was feasible, and I thought it might be. *Okay,* I thought, *I need to take a trip out there.*

By that time Gail and I had moved our family to Colorado, so I did more homework and found out that the closest airport to Death Valley was in Las Vegas. I booked a ticket and flew to Las Vegas. It was around 1990.

I rented a car and drove northwest out of Vegas on highway 95, then turned west onto 267, also known as Scotty's Castle Road. I arrived at Scotty's Castle, a famous landmark about three miles outside the park's entrance, and reset my odometer. "Okay, Lord," I prayed, "what do You want me to do?"

I drove west and then south toward Furnace Creek. From there I took Badwater Road into Badwater Basin. I wanted to see the lowest point in North America.

At Badwater I got out of my car and looked around. The place was covered with miles and miles of salt flats. Badwater Basin gets its name from a small spring-fed pool of "bad water," made bad, or undrinkable, by the surrounding salt flats. I can assure you, it is not a life-giving place. I wept as I associated one of the lowest places on Earth with the lowest place one could get in life.

I climbed back into my car and continued south on Badwater Road. Perhaps intrigued by the name, I turned east onto Jubilee Pass Road.

When my odometer read one hundred miles, I stopped the car. "Lord," I prayed, "did I miss You? Am I even supposed to be here, or is this some crazy wild-goose chase?"

"Go one more mile," a quiet voice spoke to my heart.

I dutifully pulled the car back onto the road and continued up a hill. As I curved to the right at the top of the grade, my heart leaped inside me at the sight of a sign at the side of the road: "Jubilee Pass."

Jubilee! I had driven through the lowest point on North America, and now I had reached the height of a mountain pass called Jubilee—a term the Bible uses to describe a celebration of freedom and joy for those who had been enslaved: "You shall consecrate the fiftieth year, and proclaim liberty throughout all the land to all its inhabitants. It shall be a Jubilee for you; and each of you shall return to his possession, and each of you shall return to his family" (Leviticus 25:10). If I knew anything, I knew God was speaking to me.

I went home and organized our first annual 101-mile walk through Death Valley to raise funds for children who were orphaned and abandoned. JOY International would go on to host that walk annually for the next ten years.

Nine people joined us on the first walk. The group walked twenty miles a day for five days. After a long day's walk, each evening drivers came to pick us up and take us to the Furnace Creek Ranch, where we stayed each night.

The last day of the walk we called "Breakfast at Badwater." We reached that dry, desolate place at sunrise. We ate breakfast there, and I shared a few thoughts with these people who were fighting with me to help the lowest of the low.

"Psalm 23:4 tells us that when we 'walk through the valley of the shadow of death,' we should not be afraid, because God is with us. We are now standing on the lowest spot in North America. But think about those children we are walking for. What lower place could a person be in life than to be orphaned and abandoned? Those kids cannot walk out of their valley of death— they will be freed only if someone goes in and brings them out. We can easily walk out of this low place, but they need us to lift them out of theirs. What we're going to do now, on the last day of this walk, is walk those children out of their valley of death. We aren't walking for ourselves—we're walking for them."

A solemn group rose up and set out on the last day of the walk.

At the end of the day, tired and hot from twenty miles of walking for the fifth day in a row, imagine the excitement when we climbed to the top of that pass and rounded the final bend to see that sign: "Jubilee Pass." I can tell you, everyone was unquestionably jubilant.

The funds we raised not only went to children in need of homes and families in countries around the world, but it also went to help families that were adopting internationally. One of the most powerful stories that came out of the Death Valley walks had to do with a family who walked with us on our first year, Bruce and Claudia Porter and their young children, Naomi and Jesse. Several years later our walk was specifically focused on helping the Porters raise funds to adopt their little girl, Hannah Meilan, from China. It was a success.

The year after we walked for the Porters, they returned to walk with us again—this time with baby Hannah. But what really moved me to tears was when, some twenty years later, Hannah traveled with me and a team from JOY International (led by her sister, Naomi) on a missions trip to Cambodia to minister to children and teens who were formerly enslaved. I can't begin to describe the emotion I felt at seeing our ministry come full circle with a child in that way.

The Children of Beslan

On September 3, 2004, my friend Bruce Porter (Hannah's father) contacted me. This was the day the horrific three-day Beslan school siege in Russia ended. Armed militants had held about 2,100 people captive and murdered 334 of them. The devastating news had rocked the world. "Jeff, I'm going to go there to see if I can help in some way. Would you like to go with me to see if you can do some ministry with the kids?"

I agreed to go. I felt this would be an awkward place to clown, with the sadness and trauma these children had gone through with parents and friends blown up right next to them—not to mention that I had retired from doing Snuggles in the late 1990s due to health issues. But I didn't need to wear makeup or a clown suit to minister to people as Snuggles.

When we arrived, Bruce, his son, Jesse, and I went to the school first. It was a nightmare. We literally saw body parts of children on the walls and smelled the stench of the burned-out gymnasium where the children and their parents had been held hostage by Chechen terrorists. From there we went to the hospital ward to see the injured children.

We had brought hundreds of beanie babies and other treats. As Snuggles, I had kept my Snuggles pocket circus in my huge clown pockets. I did the same thing now but without a clown suit, pulling tricks and toys from pockets just as Jeff Brodsky. I wasn't necessarily trying to make these children smile but rather simply get their minds off what they had just experienced. It was horrendous.

One little girl reminded me of the little boy in India I couldn't make smile. She was oblivious to me being there. It was as though she was looking right through me. A lot of these children were in shock. But when we handed them the beanie babies, many of the children embraced them. Some of the children loved our visit, especially when I did a magic trick for them.

Sometimes God leads us to places we never imagined going—places we never imagined even existed. During the first twenty-five years of JOY International, He led me from Disneyland to the UN building on a bicycle, to Death Valley, to Beslan, and to many other places. Now He was about to take me into a dark world I had never imagined—a place where my heart would break but where I would be motivated to give the rest of my life to rescuing people from its evil clutches.

7

Seven Seconds of Terror

I think slavery is the next thing to hell.
If a person would send another into bondage,
he would, it appears to me,
be bad enough to send him into hell if he could.

HARRIET TUBMAN

Throughout Scripture God led His people to difficult unknown places where they could share His heart with others. I think of Daniel and the Hebrews exiled to Babylon. God took this young man on a journey to a foreign land and used his obedience to reveal His glory. Then there's Joseph, sold into slavery by his brothers and taken to Egypt. Joseph's remarkable story is all about God's glory shining through Joseph's life as God used him, ultimately, to save His people. God had a plan for me to go to unknown difficult places as well, and one night He called me, loudly and clearly.

It was 2005. Gail and I were watching television one night when a documentary set in Svay Pak, Cambodia, a Vietnamese village in a district of Phnom Penh notorious for child prostitution, came on the screen. *Dateline* with Chris Hansen showed one horrific scene after another of little girls who were enslaved in child trafficking and the child sex trade. My heart broke for these children living in a country I had not yet visited.

The documentary showed children as young as five years old offering the "service" of oral sex to a group of undercover men for thirty dollars. They used childlike terms—"boom boom" and "yum yum"—to distinguish between intercourse and oral sex, respectively. Clearly, these innocent children had been taught these English language words. I grew angrier and angrier, my stomach sickened to the core.

When the documentary was over, I turned to Gail and through tears told her, "With all the travel I do around the world to help children, how can this be happening without me knowing about it? How could I possibly have been this blind?"

I couldn't believe that a man, or any human for that matter, could hear those blatantly sexual words coming out of a child's mouth and not be appalled. Even worse was the way the innocence of these children had been stolen. They offered themselves to the undercover men like it meant nothing—casually standing there, talking and giggling, like they were playing with other children in the neighborhood.

Need to Know

That documentary started me on a journey of discovery. I read everything I could get my hands on to learn as much about this travesty as possible. I had to know if this horror was actually happening and, if it was, what I could do to stop it. As I researched, I discovered that the sexual exploitation of children was, in fact, much worse than I had known or imagined. That documentary revealed the extent to which children were being abused in just one little town in Cambodia. I quickly realized that this vile injustice was happening to *millions* of children all over the world.

I went on what grew to be an insatiable quest for knowledge about the commercial sexual exploitation of children (CSEC, an official term that refers to a range of crimes involving the sexual abuse or exploitation of a child for the financial benefit of any person or in exchange for anything of value).[1] People who saw me back then would probably say I became obsessed with learning as much as I could about this heinous crime. The thought that children were being abused in this degrading and despicable manner completely overwhelmed me. I saw it (and still see it) as the most vile and loathsome crime ever perpetrated against any child since the dawn of creation—by far the worst and most evil atrocity an adult could inflict on a child.

I pored over every article, news report, and bit of information I could find. Each new statistic drove me to search for additional information to develop whatever tools were necessary to fight this horror. I searched especially for anyone who was actually focused on finding and rescuing abused children. So many people were only talking about it; I wanted to see action. I wanted to know that children were in fact being rescued and set free.

My Turning Point

For as far back as I can remember, I have slept, on average, about four hours a night. I normally wake up somewhere between two and three each morning. I seem to be hardwired for minimal sleep, as I somehow wake up feeling rested. During the fervor and intensity of my research into the CSEC, I went to bed one night emotionally exhausted.

What I'm about to share with you is deeply personal—something I rarely share with anyone. In fact, I've really wrestled with the decision to write about it. I believe that God speaks to us in many different ways, especially when He calls us to uncomfortable places. You may be able to tell your own stories of how God has gotten your attention in unconventional ways. In order for you to fully grasp why I'm so strongly driven to rescue sex-trafficked children, I share this incident—what I believe was a divine encounter—to give some perspective.

That night around two, I woke up shaking and weeping so uncontrollably that I woke up my wife.

"Jeff, what's wrong?" Gail was frightened.

I couldn't speak clearly. Through my tears I managed to choke out, "I need to go and pray."

I wasn't sure if what I had just experienced was real or a dream. I shuffled into the living room, unable to stop weeping, and paced the floor. I couldn't erase from my thoughts what had just awakened me. Even years later, as I write these words, being taken back to that moment of fear draws me to tears.

Several hours later Gail came into the living room and gently asked what had happened. The tears began to flow once more. "Gail, I don't know if it was real or a dream, but for about seven seconds God gave me the emotion of what a child feels while he or she is being ravaged. I don't know how to put it into words. It was the most horrible, excruciating thing I have ever felt."

Silence filled the room.

"Gail, my life as I know it is over," I told her. "As long as I know there are children going through the pain and suffering I felt for those few seconds, I will devote the rest of my life to rescuing as many as I can."

I have ministered in churches of just about every denomination imaginable. Since 1976, when I began my walk through life as a Messianic Jew, I have learned that spiritual perspectives vary from one person to the next, and often people's differences are based on personal experience. If you don't believe that divine healing is possible, all it takes to instantly change your theology is to experience divine healing from some sickness or witness someone being divinely healed. If you don't believe in miracles, witness one taking place and again—instant belief. My personal turning point occurred that night as God turned my intellectual understanding into an emotional imperative.

The Seven Seconds

Over my decades in the church, I've heard people pray for special gifts from God. Mostly people ask God for gifts of miracles, physical healing, or prophecy. I have begged God to give me a different gift. I have pleaded with Him to allow me to communicate to people, preferably men, what I felt for those seven seconds so that they too can feel it. I imagine women would generally have a better empathetic sense of what it might feel like to be ravaged, abused, and exploited. Men also suffer exploitation and abuse, but for the most part, it is men who perpetrate such evils on others.

If God gave me the ability to transmit the horror I felt, I could raise up an army of people to rescue these children—an army that would know what these children feel not just for seven seconds but multiple times a day. Sometimes between *ten and twenty times every day*.

If I used mere words to describe my experience, the most vivid phrase would be "brutal agony." After agony would be "nausea"—the sensation of wanting to vomit from revulsion and gagging. The next would be "terror," but what I felt goes beyond even terror. I felt a sense of horror and of suffocation, as though I was in danger of dying, unable to breathe. Seven seconds can feel like a lifetime when you're being choked, and there was nothing I could do to stop the feeling. The agony, nausea, revulsion, terror, and suffocation built up cumulatively, leading to a sense of extreme helplessness added to hopelessness.

Each sensation I experienced went beyond descriptive words. The final sensation of hopelessness was one of complete and utter despair. No one could do anything to help me; I was alone and being ferociously savaged. The sensation of fear was that of being in the grip of stark terror, trapped in the inescapable clutches of extreme evil. The sensation of agony was utterly horrific.

I thank God that it lasted only seven seconds. I'm not sure I could have handled it any longer. Every time I think about it, my mind flashes to one of those children held captive, knowing that her experience of hell on Earth extends way beyond seven seconds.

The Least at Last

Many years have now passed since this experience that changed the course of my life. It took years before I could share it with anyone besides Gail. When I did, I could hardly get the story out, overwhelmed as I was with emotion and worried that people weren't going to believe me. These days I don't really care whether or not people believe me; what I do care about is rescuing these children. I *know* what I have been called to do, and I share this message to recruit more soldiers into this war.

Apart from recognizing that the perpetrators of these crimes serve an evil master, I also realized that I had finally found the epitome of those people Jesus had referenced in Matthew 25. Children who are being used as sex slaves for commercial profit must surely epitomize what Jesus meant when He spoke about the least of these—the hungry, thirsty, stranger, naked, sick, in prison. While I realize that Christians differ theologically as to who "the least of these are" and whether these words apply to believers only or to any people we come across in this world, the Lord used this phrase to capture my attention and called me to minister Christ to children trapped in the sex-trade industry. There can be no group of people on this planet more needy and pitiable than these innocent children. I believe Jesus was speaking about these children and calling His church to enter the darkness where they live. I'll tell you why.

During Jesus' ministry on Earth, He traveled throughout Jerusalem and Judea. But the farthest north He ventured was to a region of Caesarea Philippi. It was the only time He went to this northeast region of Israel. And it was a strategic trip. He took His disciples to a renowned center of immorality. In fact, taking the disciples there would have been equivalent to taking them into a red-light district.

In the Old Testament this region was known as the center of Baal worship, and in the Roman period, it was where people made child sacrifices to the god Pan. The most deviant sexual rituals were performed to summon Pan. The site was literally known as "the gates of Hades."

The disciples would have clearly understood the significance of Jesus' statement in this place. He took them to the most morally corrupt place—and *this* is where He laid out a clear message: "You are Peter, and on this rock I will build My church, and the gates of *Hades shall not prevail against it*" (Matthew 16:18).

Here, on this rock, the Lord's church will be established. *Here*, where the rocks are carved with false gods, He asked His disciples, "Who do you say that I am?" (Matthew 16:15). *Here*, He first revealed that He was the Christ. *Here*, in this seemingly God-forsaken place, He emphatically declared that there was *no* place that His presence and power could not transform, and it was *here* that He commissioned His disciples to build His church.

In the most corrupt, morally bankrupt site in Israel, Jesus commissioned His disciples *to confront and challenge the enemy on his ground*.[2]

Jesus knew that the only way a child or young woman held as a sex slave in a brothel could hear His gospel was if He called His church to the least of these.

When I started JOY International, I could find very few who were going into these places to tell these children about Jesus. Were these dark places where children are kept captive too evil, too filthy, too dangerous for the average God-fearing person to know about or actually travel to and preach about the love of Jesus? With no one to bring light into this darkness, children were enslaved until they died or were no longer desirable, at which point they were either sold to a "lower" brothel or tossed into the street like trash.

At this stage, according to the myriad of people I've talked to over the years who are fighting this evil, one of several things usually happens. These young girls or boys simply commit suicide—overdosing on drugs, stepping into the path of a speeding vehicle, slitting their wrists—or they go into survival mode and do whatever it takes to stay alive, usually becoming prostituted. Often they simply die of exposure in the streets or from disease.

No human being should have to endure a life like this. Especially not a child. Especially not Jesus' least of these. I knew I had to do something to intercede and take action. But little did I know that this new journey would take me into the darkest corners of the countries I had already visited as Snuggles. This time, however, I would not be wearing a clown nose or floppy shoes as I traversed Thailand, India, and Cambodia. I was embarking on a new, much riskier adventure that would require me to take on new roles and use new tools.

I had found what I believed to be the least of these. Now the work had to begin.

PART 2

THE
FIGHT
FOR
THE
LEAST

8

Undercover

The secret to happiness is freedom—and the secret to freedom is courage.
THUCYDIDES

Looking at her, she seemed more like twenty than seventeen. Her long jet-black hair fell over her brown eyes and lightly tanned skin. She was one of more than twenty young girls in what are often referred to in Thailand as KTVs, an abbreviation for Karaoke Television. Literally thousands of karaoke clubs and dance bars are the rage in Thailand.

Sumana wasn't excited to be sitting next to the only out-of-shape grandpa in the room. Mamasan (the older woman in charge) had made the assignment. This young, beautiful girl was obviously thinking, *Oh, great! I'm stuck with the old fat guy!* When men enter these places, the girls usually approach male clients within seconds of their being seated. They sit close to the men and immediately start working them, encouraging them to buy drinks and snack foods—often a Thai delicacy of roasted crickets or worms. (Yes, I have eaten both.) But until Sumana was assigned to me, no girl had approached me.

As she took the seat next to mine and made an awkward attempt at conversation, the look of dismay on her face seemed to say, "Let's just go to a room and get this over with." Little did she know that I had absolutely no intention of acting like a typical client.

What If I Fail?

My undercover work in Thailand had started on a previous trip with an undercover team working to bring girls out of brothels. I didn't know the guys on the team too well—I had found them online through early exhaustive research on Google and initiated contact by e-mail. Now we were meeting for the first time, and they were going to show me their work.

We began the first night with two of the team members, both Thai nationals, giving me a driving lesson followed by a ninety-minute motorcycle ride through the countryside on our way to visit various towns in search of girls we could hopefully rescue. During the ride a vast array of emotions coursed through me. The countryside was serenely beautiful as we traveled through small villages and skirted rice paddies. It was difficult, however, to fully enjoy the stunning flora and fauna of Thailand, a country known as the Land of Smiles. My team and I were the only ones standing between these underage girls continuing a life of hell or starting the process of their liberation that evening.

Anger and fear surfaced as I thought about the world of sordid darkness I was headed toward—a sharp contrast to the scenic world whizzing by me. As I prayed, I was strengthened in the knowledge that Jesus has already invaded and conquered the darkness. I took comfort in Yeshua's victory over the lust of the flesh and over the perverted sexual depravities that drove men to abuse children.

We arrived in the town where we would be searching for underage girls in bars and brothels. This night our search would include those older girls who had no hope of escaping lives of prostitution. Many of them had been forced into sexual slavery, often while still minors. We checked into a local hotel and, after freshening up after our ride, set out on our investigation.

Walking into that first KTV, a wave of fear rose up within me. A number of questions flitted through my mind: *Can I really handle this, or will my emotions overwhelm me? What if I see a small child? Will I become incensed and enraged, or will I fall to my knees sobbing?* The other question railing around the gray outskirts of my male brain was more disturbing: *What if some of these girls who are trained to entice and seduce men manage to overpower my senses, weakening my will to resist? Am I strong enough to withstand that?*

Granted, Gail was praying for me and encouraging me to pursue this unique call on my life, even though we were more than ten thousand miles apart. But as a man, what if I failed? Without question, that was my greatest fear.

Thankfully, my fears died in the first KTV we entered. This confirmation of God's hand upon me gave me greater strength in the second one and radically empowered me in the third. Not once was I even tempted to think about anything inappropriate during the eight hours we spent visiting one brothel after another. Not once! Thank God!

On the contrary, the prayers of friends around the world strengthened me in ways I cannot begin to describe. My only thought concerning any of the girls before me became a fervent plea to God for help: *My God, please, please help me set them free. Help me free them from the hellish bondage they live in. Empower them to come to an understanding of Your perfect love.*

Undercover and Dismayed

We visited several bars and KTVs that first night. Many of the girls who worked in these places had been lied to and manipulated to participate. Others were indentured slaves, often sent to brothels by their parents in exchange for money that the girls were expected to "repay." With the high interest these debts accrued, they could rarely be repaid, so the girl was stuck there, serving in forced prostitution. The women who were manipulated into bar work were "encouraged" to have sex with clients, while those who were kept as slaves were forced to do this work. In many of the places we visited that night, I saw girls who looked as young as twelve years old.

After that night I realized I probably wasn't long for the team I was working with on that inaugural visit. The team leader, let's call him Marcus, never actually shared with me in detail about his methods or rescue plan. Instead, he instructed me simply to follow his lead. He told me I should just talk to the girl who sat next to me, hold her hand, rub her back.

Huh? was my first incredulous thought. Something didn't seem right.

I sat watching the other three men on the team. They appeared relaxed, making small talk with the girls assigned to them while either holding their hands or resting a hand on their thighs. I tried to follow their lead, since they were supposedly the experts, but it felt *very* wrong. Meanwhile, the three team members slipped seamlessly into the scene, even going up on stage to sing karaoke. (Note: In all the years I did these rescues, I made it a point of *never* going to a room alone with a girl. Even one false accusation against me could destroy many years of work.)

I understood that Marcus's team was trying to make inroads to help these girls, but I just couldn't follow through with their methods. Their strategy was simply not clear to me. In hindsight I realize they had no strategy. Throughout the several days I spent going out with this team on this first trip, I never once witnessed them rescue a girl.

I left Thailand discouraged. *There has to be a better way!* I thought. On the thirty-hour flight home, all I could think about was how I could create an actual rescue strategy. There had to be something I could do that would bring credible results without having to compromise my integrity or morals.

A Better Way

One thing I learned on that first journey is that the older girls (aged seventeen to twenty-five) are often given what appears to be a choice of either staying in the brothel or leaving when they come of age. Sadly, even though they are told they have a choice, many of them think that staying on as sex workers is actually their only option. They have no hope that there is anything better for them.

After years of experience, JOY International is committed to doing everything we can to help the older girls decide to leave their lives of prostitution. We explain to them that they will be taken to a safe house where they will receive counseling and opportunities to find decent jobs while having their dignity restored. We help with funding so they can receive educations or learn trades. The difficult part is convincing them to verbally say, "Yes, I want to leave here." It sometimes takes many visits to the same KTV or dance bar building trust with these girls to achieve this breakthrough.

I also realized on that first trip that these girls can be physically aggressive when we enter a KTV or bar. I needed something, a tool that would help me take control of the situation. I've learned (and now live according to this understanding) that if you aren't in control, situations have the potential to spiral out of control.

As I considered a strategy that would give me necessary control and help me break down barriers of mistrust—without compromising my morals and integrity—I had an idea that brought me back to my days as Snuggles the Love Clown and the reactions from people as I did my close-up magic tricks. When I stood in the street and did close-up magic routines, it would gather a crowd of children and their parents (sometimes in the hundreds) and grab their attention. Although I had retired from clowning many years earlier, my memories of it sparked a thought: *What a great way to take complete control and build relationship by bringing out the true child in each girl or young woman, even in a bar or KTV.*

Still, I had no idea if it would work.

Before I left America for my second trip to Thailand, I brushed up on a wide range of close-up magic tricks and illusions. I could even throw fire out of my hand—always an attention getter!

I went back to Thailand a couple months after my first trip, and, not having a new team to work with, I decided to work undercover with Marcus and his team again. I hoped to show them a better way this time.

So now I sat in the KTV where the mamasan had assigned Sumana to me. Would my new plan work?

9

Here Goes Nothing

Laughter is the shortest distance between two people.
VICTOR BORGE

As I sat in the loud, dimly lit KTV with Sumana, she placed her hand on my thigh. To her surprise I immediately removed it and placed the bag that held my assortment of tricks on my leg instead. I reached into the bag, took a deep breath, and thought to myself, *Here goes nothing. Let the fun begin.* I hoped and prayed.

Unable to speak her language, I gestured to Sumana to hold out her hand. The quizzical look on her face was priceless—she had no idea what to expect. I took her hand and placed a red sponge ball in her palm. Then I closed her hand, did some fancy hand waving over her fist, and voila! The red ball changed to a black one! Sumana squealed with delight, and all heads in the room turned to see what was happening. Suddenly the focus was on the old grandpa who looked like Santa Claus.

I took the black ball, placed it back in her hand, and did more hocus-pocus hand waving over her closed fist. When she opened it, she was hysterical with laughter and excitement to see not one but three red balls! Childlike innocence peeked through her eyes. By that time, the vibe in the entire room had changed. I gathered up all three balls and put them back in her hand, once again waving my hands over hers. This time when she opened her hand, they were gone!

Next I showed Sumana and the growing crowd of girls my magic coloring book. I turned the pages, revealing nothing but blank white pages. Through an interpreter on our team, I told Sumana I would turn her fingers into magic crayons. She smiled big, her eyes sparkling. If only for a few minutes, her stolen childhood seemed within reach.

I asked Sumana to use her finger to scribble all over the outside of the book. Then I opened the once blank book, revealing page after page of black-and-white pictures. The girls screamed with delight. I closed the book, and this time I asked her to use all her fingers to scribble on the cover. All the black-and-white pictures were suddenly turned to beautiful full color.

At this point all the girls, including the mamasan, were laughing. Everyone in the room had packed in closely together, surrounding us. My team members were astonished by what I was doing and how I had taken complete control of the room.

I announced to Sumana that I would turn her hand into a magical eraser, and you guessed it, after she waved her hand over the book, I opened it to reveal blank white pages once again. All the pictures had disappeared! Amazed, Sumana wanted to figure out how the pictures kept changing and disappearing. She insisted on holding the magic coloring book herself. When I handed it to her, she opened it and was astonished to see that all the pages were black and white again. When she handed it back to me, I opened it, and all the color pictures were back! Everyone laughed again. Even the stern mamasan gave a hearty chuckle.

This Guy Is Different

In just a few minutes, I had changed this seventeen-year-old girl's perception of me. She looked at me with a gaze that said, *This old guy may not be too cute, but he saw something deep in me, and he is really fun. He even made me feel special in front of all the other girls.* In her face I saw the pressure, horror, and pain of spending years in that brothel slowly fade as light invaded darkness and joy replaced oppression.

I continued performing one illusion after another, each one building on the rapport I sensed developing between me and Sumana and the rest of my audience. Relationship erased mistrust, just like my "magic" erased the pictures in my coloring book. Although I was focused on Sumana, the magic tricks were not just for her. I was there for each enslaved girl in this KTV.

When it was time to leave, I set up my final trick. I wanted to make a statement. In Thai culture it's customary to tip the girl with whom you've spent the evening, even if you didn't have sex with her. By now Sumana had no doubt begun to wonder, *Is he going to take me to a room now? Am I going to have to perform for him to receive a tip?*

I surprised everyone when I asked her to give me a one-hundred-baht note (equivalent to about three U.S. dollars). Visibly shocked by my request, she went ahead and handed me a note. With everyone watching intently and listening carefully, I slowly folded the hundred-baht note inches from her face. The interpreter relayed to Sumana the words I spoke: "Sumana, I really enjoyed meeting you, and I want to thank you for spending this time with me. You are a beautiful girl and so very special. I believe your time is much more valuable than this one hundred baht. You are precious and valuable, created by God for a much greater purpose than what you do here."

As I spoke, I unfolded the now minuscule hundred-baht note. As the note slowly unfurled, it dawned on Sumana that it had somehow transformed into a *one-thousand*-baht note! Gasps filled the room.

I handed it to her and thanked her again. In amazement, astonishment, and gratitude this young girl stared sweetly at me, smiling widely.

I Want to Leave This Place

As I made my way to the door, the unexpected happened. All the girls had gathered at the entrance. They wanted to hug me but in a tender, grateful way. I desperately fought back tears. Before I walked out, the stern mamasan came over to me and, addressing me in broken English, said, "I never meet a man like you. *Never!* Thank you so much for what you do. You are very special man. You have very big heart. You please come back here any time." Then she stepped forward and added her hug to the many I had already received.

With tears flowing, I just about ran out of there. How could I leave behind Sumana and several other girls who could not have been more than fifteen or sixteen years old—knowing the kind of life they would return to that night?

I waited outside for the rest of the team, wondering what was taking them so long to come out. Later I learned that the girls had been asking questions like, "Who was that man who looked like Santa Claus?" and "Why did he come here?" My new ministry strategy had saved our team a whole lot of time. Typically exposing their true function to the girls took a long time, even months. That night they were able to open up and explain the reason for their presence before we left.

One of the girls spoke those beautiful words I so long for— words I have dedicated my life to hearing.

"I want to leave this place," she told one of our team members. "I want to go and live at the safe house."

It was Sumana.

This beautiful young girl had never expected to hear that night that she was valuable, loved, and prized by God. My heart soared with joy at being used by God as a tool to break a prisoner's chains and free a captive from a web of bondage. Janis Joplin sang the words "Freedom's just another word." I disagree with Ms. Joplin. Freedom is not just another word. It is a hope, a prayer. It is an absolute right for every human being. For Sumana it was life.

Freedom for all begins with those of us who are already free. How many more girls like Sumana are waiting for someone to come to them and break their chains? How many captives still pray for the joy of freedom?

Let me share a little haiku I wrote (I began writing haiku when I met my wife and am currently in the process of writing a haiku for every page of the Bible):

Following God's call
To set another child free
Oh, the JOY it brings

From that night on, I knew that the close-up magic I had learned to draw a crowd and share the gospel would be my calling card each time I went undercover and talked to a girl enslaved in a brothel. I had found a better way. I knew I had turned a corner in my life. I would be unstoppably zealous in following this call that God had given me and would spend my life fighting this gross injustice against His precious children. God had miraculously changed my vision. I no longer saw exploited girls with the eyes of a man. Instead I saw them through the eyes of God.

To this day I have never seen a girl in need of rescue in quite the same way. I have never had the slightest thought of lust, only a father's heart with an intense longing to set these captives free and watch them flourish through the love of God.

My first undercover experiences introduced me to a new form of evil I had never encountered before. But little did I know that I would soon come face to face with an almost tangible darkness that few people ever confront firsthand.

10

Fifty Failures

There is no such thing as freedom without the risk of failure.
GOVERNOR RICK PERRY

Our team had started working at ten in the morning. It was now one in the morning the next day—fifteen hours later—and we were exhausted! I was working with Indian Rescue Mission, which included five nationals and myself. We were in Mumbai, one of the largest cities in the world, and had been on the go, virtually nonstop, for several days. We had traveled from one brothel to the next, some places thinly disguised as dance bars, others brazenly displaying their human wares.

I was grateful for the earplugs I had stashed in my bag. In the first dance bar, the music was so loud that I couldn't hear any of the team members, even though they were shouting directly into my ear. The endless thump, thump, thump of the bass combined with the high-pitched vocals mutilated my then fifty-five-year-old ears. Louder than any concert I had ever been to, the noise was truly deafening! Before long I realized why the music was so loud and incessant—to mask the noises coming from the rooms where girls were being ravaged. The realization sickened me.

Although these establishments were called dance bars, very few people actually danced. Instead men sat at tables, and the girls simply stood in the middle of the room, as if posing, while the men ogled them. Any attempt to photograph one of the girls with a camera or phone drew immediate attention from one of the well-dressed, tuxedo-clad housemen who were there, in part, to prevent clients from capturing any images. To circumvent the rules and get the evidence we needed, I pretended to talk on my phone or show pictures to other team members while I was actually snapping pictures of underage girls.

In the dance bars, if a client was interested in a girl, he either motioned for her to join him or instructed a young male host to send her over. When they entered the place, men usually exchanged American dollars for Indian rupees. Most asked for stacks of ten-rupee notes. Back then, at the exchange rate of sixty rupees to one U.S. dollar, fifty dollars would buy a stack of three hundred ten-rupee notes. To show interest in a girl, clients simply handed a stack of bills to one of the men on the floor, who then made a show of the bills, fanning them out and briskly flicking the bills with his thumb over the head of the designated girl. This crass and ostentatious gesture was to signify the man's opulence. Literally "raining" rupees onto her head entitled the man to start a conversation with the girl.

Conversing with these young girls was a challenge for me not only due to the language barrier but also because of the loud music. In places where the girls spoke English, they sauntered over to me and tried to attract my attention; the bolder ones actually initiated conversation. But no matter who initiated conversation in these bars, however, even without taking a girl to a room, men were still expected to tip a girl for the time she spent talking with them—similar to the tradition in the KTVs in Thailand.

Our team members followed a strict rule: at no point were we allowed to take a girl into a room, especially alone. This was the golden rule, rigorous and inflexible, and it applied to all of us. To prevent placing myself or any other team member in a compromising position, we *always* went out in teams of two or more men. Now I think that's part of the reason Jesus sent the disciples out in twos—to ensure strict accountability.

When one of our team members noticed an obviously underage girl, he started a conversation with her. If a team member suspected that a girl was not only underage but also being held against her will, he set the video function on his hidden camera to "Record" and led her out of the room, away from the noise. Asking a few specific questions quickly revealed if she was being held against her will. In addition to her age, he asked why she was working in a dance bar and who had brought her there. He also asked if she wanted to be there and whether or not she was easily able to leave whenever she chose. Then he asked her if she wanted to leave the brothel to be taken to a safe house. If she agreed to the help he offered, he made plans for a potential rescue. If the girl was obviously a minor (there's a limit to how much makeup can age a twelve-year-old), he took the video footage to the police to schedule a raid.

We faced challenges with raids too. For one, these dance bars had men stationed as lookouts outside. If they saw police approaching, they signaled their boss, who then rushed the underage girls out a back or side door. It was just another stake that drove home the sickening reality of the situation.

Whenever I went undercover with James Varghese and his team at the Indian Rescue Mission, JOY International financed the operation. In fact, this was how JOY International worked—we looked for people already doing rescue work in various countries, and then we supported them with finances, practical help, partnership, or in any way we could. While I felt much better about working with this team than the Thai one, at first it concerned me to see team members using money that our ministry had provided to buy drinks and food. It especially bothered me to watch them showering the girls with rupees. After witnessing the system firsthand though, I soon realized that this was a necessary evil and crucial to maintaining our cover. Trained team members were posing as customers, and they did what customers did. A little spending money gave them the opportunity to engage young girls in necessary conversation. It also made it easier to spot the girls who were underage or being held against their will (we could read facial expressions and body language as if they were an unspoken language). Without these funds rescues would have been practically impossible.

Various Venues

I noticed distinct differences between dance bars, KTVs, and brothels.

When a man went into a dance bar or KTV, he might just have been there to spend some time with friends, drinking and ogling the girls. He might have been looking for more. Both dance bars and KTVs were fronts for prostitution.

The dance bars had a festive atmosphere with loud music, flashing lights, and girls parading around in either skimpy or classy outfits. There was also a visible flow of cash being flashed around, enticing girls to pay particular attention to big spenders. At KTVs, instead of dancing the girls sang on stage (really just so they could be seen). The customers (especially after a few drinks) also went up and sang too. KTVs were not popular in India, but I learned that they were everywhere in places like Thailand and Cambodia and all across Southeast Asia.

The brothels had a completely different vibe. Run according to strict business principles, they had no music, no dark rooms with flashing lights, and no attendants in tuxedos. The places were usually divided into a selection of bedrooms situated at the back, out of sight, with one or more viewing rooms near the entrance. A brothel was solely about sex. There were times, of course, when a man visited a brothel and left without taking a girl into a room.

That's what our teams did every time. We simply gave the impression that we were looking for the right girl. Many men shopped this way, visiting one brothel after another until they made a choice. Then they went back to the brothel housing the girl they had decided upon.

Whether our team visited dance bars, KTVs, or brothels, we were searching either for underage girls or girls who were being held against their will. It was extremely heartbreaking when we discovered a girl in desperate need of rescue but were unable to simply set her free and walk out the door with her. Exiting a place while knowing full well we were leaving a precious girl or young woman behind brought inexplicable guilt.

Being forced to turn our backs on people in such desperate need was gut-wrenchingly difficult. Every time we had to walk away, biding our time until we could arrange to have the girl rescued, we were tormented by the knowledge she would have to service an untold number of men until our return. I quickly discovered that this was one of the worst aspects of doing this work. Having to stand by and wait for the police to organize a raid, knowing how the girls were suffering, tore me apart.

Like a Pimp

The night I realized why the music in some dance bars was so loud was part of my first rescue operation in India. I was grateful to finally be participating in work that could actually make a difference in the lives of these girls and young women.

The next afternoon I got ready to head to a brothel with two operative team members, Viraj and Dastigir (I called him Dusty for short). Our mission that evening was to search brothels for underage girls, using a hidden camera so we could later prove our findings.

Sitting in a restaurant prior to heading out, I looked at Viraj. His shirt was an attention-getter. It had a metallic-gold sheen to it, and Viraj had unbuttoned the top few buttons to reveal some of his chest. As we crowded into the rickshaw, I chirped, "You know, Viraj, you look like a pimp."

Viraj's eyebrows crashed together as he frowned at me.

"You think I look like pimp?"

His classic Indian accent, gleaming gold shirt, and the edge of shock in his voice that I could even suggest such a thing were reminiscent of a scene from a Bollywood movie.

"Yes," I said, "you look like pimp!"

"Why you think I look like pimp?" he asked, partially defiant and possibly wounded.

"Look at your shiny shirt," I said, "and the way you have those top buttons undone. You're like a pimp."

Viraj glanced down at his shirt, still frowning.

"I have an idea," I continued, the smile fading. "When we arrive at the brothel, let's act out a little scenario that will make our visit more plausible. Let's make believe you're my personal pimp. I'll play the part of a wealthy American looking for young girls, and you'll be the pimp I've hired to search them out for me and find the right young girls."

I told Viraj that when we reached the brothel, he should sit next to me on the couch. Dusty was to stand next to me with his arms folded, like a bodyguard. Since Dusty wore the hidden camera, having him stand would mean he could turn his body where needed.

Viraj nodded. "I think this might work. Yes, this could definitely work."

"When we arrive," I added, "I won't speak directly to the brothel owner or the manager. I will speak only through you. We can do this?" I asked.

"Yes, I think we can do this."

We left the restaurant, and the three of us squeezed into an auto rickshaw, or what they call a *tuk tuk* in India. At a certain area we got out, paid the rickshaw driver, and started walking the streets, trying one brothel after the next in our search for underage girls.

Brothels all had a similar layout. Upon entering, clients were shown to a viewing room that usually had a coffee table, couch, and a few chairs and were then seated, facing a wall, while the women or girls were brought out on display. Four or five women lined up against the wall, facing the clients, and bright floodlights were switched on. The girls were usually numbered, but sometimes they had name tags. It made things easy for the clients, who could simply say, "I want Bala," or, "I want number twelve."

The entire process was really heart wrenching for me, because going into a viewing room, I knew that if I didn't see any underage girls, I would just dismiss the lot of them. With the wave of my hand, I could simply dismiss the entire group, as though they meant absolutely nothing. In essence, I was literally rejecting them, saying that they weren't good enough.

I could almost see the girls' thoughts spinning: *Here's this old grandpa who looks like Santa Claus, and he's rejecting me? I'm not good enough for him?* So, in some twisted way, I was causing even more pain. In some cases the dismissive wave of my hand might have had them thinking, *Oh, these rich Americans—they tip well. If only he hadn't rejected me.* And then, of course, others took one look at me and probably thought, *Thank God he rejected me!* I'm also pretty sure some of them might have wondered if I was abusive. They didn't know me from Adam. They couldn't be sure. It was a harrowing business. I could see the confusion and fear in their eyes as they played out these different scenarios in their heads.

Now, having spent so many years in rescue work, within the first thirty seconds, I'm able to discern a number of facts about these women or girls. I can see who wants to be there, who's forced to be there, whether they're new to the business or have been there for a number of years, and how experienced they are at acting out the role they perform.

A girl's eyes and hands usually give her away. Is she looking directly at me with a "pick me" type of expression? Is she looking away? Looking down? Shifting her gaze from side to side? Hands give clues too. In fact, they usually confirm what the eyes are saying. Are the girl's hands quivering? Are they glistening with sweat? Is she wringing her fingers? By observing the hands, I can learn a lot.

So Viraj, Dusty, and I ended up in a brothel in Mumbai, Viraj playing the pimp and me vociferously demanding to see young girls. During our negotiations I wasn't sure we could pull off our scheme or if they would ever bring out the younger girls. As you read in the introduction of this book, finally we saw those girls.

As we walked out of the brothel following the tense scene inside and moved a safe distance down the sidewalk, Viraj looked at me shakily. "Jeff, you scared the crap out of me! I didn't know you were going to get that crazy. I thought you were real!" The ensuing laughter broke the tension of the episode.

Sadly, the corruption of the local police department ran too deep at that time. In the end, we came up short.

Falling Short

Sadly, failed rescue missions such as the one in Mumbai became fairly common for us during our early years in India. This was one of fifty—yes, *fifty*—failed rescue attempts in a three-week period. The lack of success was gut wrenching. Every time we arrived with a task force the day after we had gathered incriminating evidence against a group of traffickers, we discovered an empty building.

Apart from the extreme disappointment at falling short of our goal, it was exhausting work with no reward. We had, in fact, spent thousands of dollars setting up these rescue operations, but the financial loss was the least disappointing aspect. We ended each day knowing that, somehow, we had failed the women and children we were working so hard to rescue.

I had to embark on a pretty steep learning curve. I found that corruption often factored into the overall equation. My early rescue missions took place during the time when famed police officer

Daya Nayak had risen to prominence in Mumbai as an "encounter specialist" for a crack response team that also inquired into trafficking reports.[1] Nayak had joined the police force in 1995 and quickly acquired a reputation as a specialist, subduing a great deal of crime in the late 1990s and early 2000s. Before his specialist police group formed and began fighting back against Mumbai's gangsters, it was difficult to apprehend any gangster implicated in human trafficking. Still, even with him and his team on the streets, the insidious links between organized crime and the corruption of police, prosecutors, and the legal system were extremely complex obstacles to negotiate. (Nayak is still at it today, putting bad guys away and making Mumbai safer for girls, and we have often partnered with his team.)

To say I was discouraged and confused would be a gross understatement. What made matters worse was the criticism we received. People accused us of wasting money. I began to realize how callous people could be.

"Really?" I asked people. "What if it was your child? Would it be a waste of money if I had been searching for your child?"

I asked God what I was doing wrong. *Why are our best-laid plans not working? Am I wasting my time, my energy, and our donors' money? Why are we not seeing results for our labor?*

God showed me that I was learning valuable lessons about what *not* to do. These discouraging experiences were part of my education. I knew what I wanted to do, but it seemed as if barely anyone else was doing it, so I had no option but to learn from my mistakes. Knowing that God had called me to do this work, I took comfort in the knowledge that each failure was bringing me closer to the first rescue that would succeed.

11

The Rescue Plan

Dum spiro, spero. (While I breath, I hope.)
LATIN PROVERB

Being an early riser, one morning at three I was at my desk in my home office in Colorado. Within a few minutes of arriving, I received a Facebook message from James with India Rescue Mission emphasizing the potential for a rescue operation. The scenario looked promising, so I agreed to finance the rescue.

Viraj, IRM's field investigator, had managed to initiate a rare contact with a woman known to be one of the most notorious child traffickers in Mumbai. The police despised this woman. For years they had been unable to locate, let alone apprehend, her, mainly due to the shrewdness she employed in her vile business. She was meticulous and exceptionally cautious. This woman trusted no one, and if she ever had any doubt about a potential trafficking deal, she simply wouldn't show up. Even the vaguest suggestion of an unorthodox deal caused her to vanish.

Viraj explained the deal being brokered by this woman pimp: Two women were planning to sell the virginity of young family members. One mother had arranged to set up her two daughters for rape in exchange for cash; one girl was fourteen years old, the other sixteen. The second woman planned to sell the virginity of her fifteen-year-old niece via the same female pimp.

Why, you may wonder, *would anyone want to buy a child in the first place?*

Over the years I've discovered various reasons. It may be a straightforward case of a pedophile's perversion, but in some cases it's more sinister, especially within certain cultures, where a twisted, superstitious mind-set takes hold. In certain parts of Asia, India, and Africa, a prevalent ideology dupes men into believing that sex with a virgin will bring them good fortune. This practice is rife among men whose businesses are failing. Losing money, they become desperate and are willing to pay hundreds, even thousands, of dollars to have sex with a virgin in the hopes that it will reverse their bad fortune. Sex with more than one virgin will supposedly bring them even more good fortune.

Sadly, there is more to this superstition. Because these businessmen of low moral repute frequently visit prostitutes, they often contract AIDS, and another twisted belief comes into play: many believe that if an infected man has sex with a virgin, he will pass his disease to the child, curing himself of AIDS. Even if that ridiculous notion were true, how vile must a man be to sacrifice the life of a child in the hope of curing himself? To pass his death sentence on to an innocent child by raping her? A child is treated as a commodity, worthless beyond the price for which she can be traded.

A Tenuous Operation

We immediately set into motion a plan to rescue all three girls and took the necessary steps to ensure that both women selling children and also the pimp would be arrested. Ultimately, it would take about six weeks of negotiation and cost a few thousand dollars with absolutely no guarantee of a successful rescue. This volatility is one of the main reasons why so few organizations are willing to pursue actual rescues.

Our more than fifty failed rescues had taught us a thing or two. When we realized why we kept failing, we instantly changed our strategy: once we were certain we had enough evidence to put criminals away, we would immediately close the net and strike the same day, while the trafficked women and children were still on the premises. That way no one would have time to make a discrete phone call to warn the perpetrators.

Our negative statistics began to change after this and also as we developed good relationships with honest law enforcement personnel. When we worked specifically with appointed police officers, our rescue rate improved dramatically. We eventually learned how to process our rescue scenarios correctly. It was a long and difficult learning process, but we implemented methods to weed out corrupt police officers. Our teams still faced many hurdles, some of which were ridiculous irregularities within the actual legal systems of specific countries. But we refused to give up.

In the new case James had brought to us, we had quite a few hurdles to overcome.

First, the female pimp crazily demanded two thousand dollars per child up front. This price gave the client the right to take the virginity of each girl he paid for and included a few bonus evenings with her. Assuming the role of a pimp who was supposedly working on behalf of a client interested in young virgin girls, Viraj began negotiations. But for a small organization like JOY International, six thousand dollars was a huge sum of money. I decided to put my negotiating skills into action without compromising the potential success of the operation; I had to do whatever it would take to change these girls' futures. After some negotiating, the pimp agreed to accept five hundred dollars as a deposit to hold all three girls until the actual "buyer" arrived. We had cleared the first inevitable hurdle.

Then we had to be sure we could raise the funds in time. The original plan was for me to pose as the so-called wealthy American who would fly to Mumbai for a week of perverse "fun." But it would take me a few weeks first to raise the funds and for the team in India to set up the sting operation, so we hoped the pimp would agree to wait. We sent the five hundred dollars to our director of operations, who handed over the money to the woman pimp. She accepted our terms.

We hit another barrier: after two weeks, the pimp contacted Viraj and told him she wasn't going to wait much longer. If she found another buyer, she would return our deposit and sell the girls' virginity elsewhere. Coordinating a rescue operation is not an exact science, and as issues presented themselves, we had to adapt. So I rearranged my schedule. I immediately booked a flight to Mumbai, but as I still did not have the full dollar amount requested, we decided to give the greedy pimp an additional deposit, which we hoped would secure the deal. Once I arrived, we paid an additional fifteen hundred dollars and explained to the pimp that she would receive the balance when we saw the girls. This appeased her for the moment.

More Difficulties

Only after my arrival did we recognize yet another problem. If I were the undercover "client" involved in the actual sting, after the rescue I would have to travel back and forth between the United States and India as a witness for the prosecution, which could drain JOY International's funds. Simply unable to afford this added expense, we set another scenario in motion: James, IRM's director, would pose as the client. Aside from a noticeable Indian accent on the day of the rescue, the difference would be undetectable to the pimp. Another hurdle was cleared, but I was getting concerned. Taking this female pimp off the streets would potentially save thousands of girls from lives of terror, humiliation, and pain. We could not afford to mess this up.

Now we had to set the day, time, and location of the exchange. Viraj decided with the female pimp that the handoff would take place at a busy restaurant in the city. I planned to be there in time to witness and capture the exchange on film with a hidden camera as evidence for the impending court case. The trafficker wanted to trade only one girl first, a young lady named Solana being sold by her aunt. We told the pimp we would trade the two sisters at another time. The trafficker expected to be present at both exchanges, but of course, we had to arrest and imprison her at the first exchange. We could not let Solana or the sisters be sold to anyone else.

The day of the planned rescue, I left the hotel with Dusty and Vikas, two other members of our team, for the rendezvous location. Our tension was palpable. We each sensed the stress within the others, knowing that one wrong decision, one flicker of suspicion on the part of the female pimp, could blow the entire operation.

The previous evening James had called us, further emphasizing how tenuous this rescue really was. He had confided in me how depressed and nervous he was, knowing from experience that all it took was one ill-fated moment for our rescue attempts to end in disaster. Sadly, he knew, as did I, how easily several weeks' worth of planning and work could be destroyed.

12

First Success

I've been staring at the world, waiting;
I've been looking for a change lately.
All the trouble and all the pain we're facing—
Someone gotta be the hope and someone gotta be the love.
BRITT NICOLE

As our taxi zigzagged its way through the sprawling city of more than twenty million people, I sensed that something was amiss. I had worked with Dusty and Vikas many times, but until that night I had never heard them argue. Clearly the pressure of the operation was taking its toll. When the taxi driver got lost not once or twice but *seven* times, it was almost more than we could handle. If we were late, the case was done. The evil pimp might still be arrested, but without video evidence, it was almost guaranteed that she would walk free. I couldn't help envisioning over and over again the entire sting operation unfolding without us being present. The night would become one of the most harrowing I had experienced since I began working with rescue operations.

Hour after hour, we stopped to ask directions again and yet again, all seven times. On top of the anxiety this produced, I thought about the thousands of dollars we had spent to reach this moment and what a major accomplishment arresting this particular woman would be in the fight against child trafficking in Mumbai. I also obsessed angrily over the depths of depravity in the aunt who was selling her own flesh and blood.

Dangerously close to the edge of my frustration, my mind suddenly snapped back to real time. James and Viraj were surely already at the designated restaurant, and here Dusty and Vikas and I were, in essentially a little motorcycle rickshaw, lost in heavy traffic. *What if we miss the entire operation? How will our court case be affected if we have no film to prove the money exchange?* I wanted to scream at the top of my lungs.

The Height of Tension

I closed my eyes and prayed, and within minutes we arrived. I wondered anxiously if we were too late. I breathed a huge sigh of relief when I noticed James still seated and alongside him Viraj. We had arrived in time.

Instantly my mind kicked into operation mode, and I noted where the team members had positioned themselves. At a table next to James and Viraj, our two plainclothes policemen were dining with their "dates," who were actually social workers. These two women were there to whisk Solana away immediately after her aunt and the trafficker were arrested. They would ensure the girl's protection and also reassure her of her safety. James posed as the pedophile client, while Viraj portrayed the child broker who was negotiating the deal for James. Dusty, Vikas, and I casually ignored James and Viraj.

Our troubles weren't over yet: since the restaurant was almost completely full, the host tried to usher us into another room. I couldn't bring too much attention to myself, but playing the entitled foreigner, I arrogantly insisted on a table in the room where our colleagues were seated. I barked at the host that I would not accept a seat in an inferior section, and the look in my eye told him I would not take no for an answer. As is the Asian way, our host congenially assured us (with no small amount of head waggling) that there was no problem and implored us to wait for seats. Still in character, I grudgingly agreed as the trafficker had not yet arrived. But I had to be in place before the deal was struck. In times like this, a simple five-dollar tip works wonders.

As usual, God's timing and attention to detail were astonishing. When the host politely escorted us to our table, the trafficker had still not arrived, and our seating arrangements were perfectly orchestrated. James and Viraj's table was clearly visible from where the two plainclothes policemen and social workers were seated, and Dusty, Vikas, and I were seated directly behind the policemen's and social workers' table. It was critical that the policemen be close enough to the table where the deal was struck to witness the exchange of money.

Things were lining up, but I was becoming physically and emotionally exhausted. *How much more can we handle?* I prayed that our stress would not be detectable to the eagle-eyed female pimp.

I suddenly wondered if this notorious trafficker would even show up. My stomach flipped. *Oh Lord, have we wasted all this time, effort, and money?*

To distract myself, I ordered some food and set up my camera—an iPad I had propped up so I could pretend to show photos to Dusty and Vikas. The next five minutes felt like an eternity. We put on our tourist smiles and waited.

Finally the trafficker showed up with the girl and her aunt. My heart hammered in my chest as the restaurant host smiled and seated the pimp, the aunt, and Solana at James's table. Solana sat in the chair to my right, so I quickly adjusted my camera, positioning myself to make sure she couldn't see the video but I could still film the entire exchange. I sighed in relief. With the woman pimp now surrounded by undercover plainclothes police, I finally felt a little confident that this girl would be rescued. We just had to wait until the money changed hands.

Pretending to look out the window, I glanced at Solana. She alternated between watching her aunt anxiously and looking down at her dress—not even reading the menu. This young lady created in God's image had no idea she was on the verge of either being saved or subjected to a dark night and life of unfathomable pain. Instantly I knew, legal case or not, that there was no way I would allow this young girl to be enslaved.

My gaze turned to the two women social workers chatting glibly with the plainclothes policemen. Their conversation continued in laughs and banter for twenty or thirty minutes, while I did my best to appear as though I was enjoying a fine Indian dinner and showing my colleagues hilarious video clips on my iPad (as it recorded).

Unexpectedly, a silence fell over Viraj's table. I saw the female pimp's eyes turn to stone as she gazed into James's eyes. Solana's aunt shifted nervously in her seat as James returned the pimp's stony stare with a smirk that was ever so slight. He then reached into his jacket's inner pocket and discreetly pushed an envelope full of cash to the middle of the table. As quickly and slyly as a snake, the pimp's hand slid across to the envelope and pulled it into her lap. The stony eyes remained fixed, but a greedy smile flickered across her lips. Anxiously I checked the angle of my iPad and the "Record" button to be sure it had captured this scene. It had.

One of the plainclothes policemen smiled and subtly turned away to make a call on his cell phone. Within ten seconds a group of uniformed police flooded the restaurant from every entrance. Witnessing the shock on the notorious female pimp's face was one of the most rewarding moments of my life. As the realization that she had finally been outwitted flashed across her face, the fear of what would follow produced a panic I pray I never experience. Solana's aunt displayed the same shock and fear. Maintaining my cover, I silently rejoiced, grinning at my two fellow operatives, and thanking our heavenly Father for moving heaven and hell to get us through all these hurdles.

It's Always Worth It

I glanced back as the two social workers sprang up to protect the thoroughly confused fifteen-year-old girl. Solana had no idea of the horror she had just been saved from as the social workers rapidly escorted her out of the restaurant. Maintaining their cover, James and Viraj feigned shock and fear too, allowing themselves to be "arrested" with the two female criminals.

I simply cannot describe the joy I felt as we watched these criminals being led away in cuffs. In that moment we knew that, with God's intercession, we had orchestrated the perfect sting operation. A flood of tension drained from my shoulders and body.

The notorious pimp was eventually sentenced to a ten-year prison term. Solana's aunt also received prison time. I thought the pimp should have been given a life sentence, as her greed had ruined the lives of so many innocent children. But I would take what I could get.

When the social workers interviewed Solana, they asked her if she knew why she had been taken to the restaurant. Solana had no idea. She told the social workers she had never been to a restaurant before and had never worn such a pretty dress.

One of the social workers broke the news to her: "Solana, you were being sold by your aunt."

"Sold? For what?"

"Solana, you were going to be sold for sex."

When I heard Solana's response, I thought my heart would crumble into a thousand pieces. "What is sex?" she asked.

Although Solana lived in a fifteen-year-old body, her mind was much less developed. She had slight mental retardation, making her aunt's profiteering plan that much more despicable.

Had she been sold to a real pedophile, Solana would have been robbed of more than just her virginity. Unable to mentally cope with what was happening to her, this young, confused girl would likely have been traumatized to a point of irrevocable terror and agony.

The two other girls the pimp had planned to sell were taken from their home and to a safe house along with Solana. The mother of these two girls was found culpable in the scheme and was also arrested and sentenced to time in prison. Considering the six weeks and thousands of dollars JOY International spent rescuing Solana and the two sisters, was it worth the results? Ask Solana. Or the two sisters. Or the innumerable girls who will never be sold into a brothel because that pimp is off the streets.

What if our rescue had failed? True, previous rescues had failed, but each failure had led to this success. *Every rescue is worth every dollar paid.* Just having that trafficker imprisoned was worth a hundred times what we spent. This was the first successful rescue operation I was involved with in Mumbai, and apart from a sense of absolute job satisfaction, it spurred me on, giving me needed encouragement to continue doing the work God had called me to do in the rescue of children from commercial sexual exploitation.

What I would eventually come to understand as I grew increasingly passionate about turning over every dark corner to find the least of these was that the heart God had given me to do His work was His own.

13

Better Off Dead

When you say a situation or a person is hopeless,
you're slamming the door in the face of God.
CHARLES L. ALLEN

For nearly forty years and in varying degrees, I've been involved in the rescue of orphaned, abused, and abandoned children. For more than ten years, I've been devoted to the rescue and restoration of children forced into the child sex trade. Without question, child sex trafficking is *the* worst crime perpetrated against children since the dawn of creation. I read horror stories about the commercial sexual exploitation of children literally every day, seven days a week. Each story of the vile abuse these children suffer is heart wrenching, but no story has angered and upset me as much as a report sent to me by our friend and co-worker in this fight against trafficking, Diana Scimone.

Diana leads the Born2Fly (B2F) Project, working to educate children and their parents about child predators. The B2F Project has written a curriculum taught by ministries all over the world where children are at risk for sex slavery, and it has been extremely effective in its efforts. JOY International is proud to support this organization. Here is a report Diana sent out:

> When I tell you that child trafficking is organized crime, I'm not kidding. Trafficking is very, very lucrative with very few risks. Organized crime has made it the second-highest grossing illegal industry on the planet.
>
> So what happens when you threaten the traffickers' livelihood? Let's say you want to cut off the supply line of kids, and let's say you teach kids and parents how to stand up to traffickers. Let's say you do this in an area where kids are regularly kidnapped and trafficked—what happens?
>
> In a village in the Philippines where our brave partners have been openly teaching the B2F Project anti-trafficking curriculum to children and their parents, . . . our Philippines director was attacked by a trafficker, who broke one of her ribs. (He was arrested.) Then this happened, as reported by the Philippines director:
>
>> One of the children we have worked with for over a year was kidnapped this week and later returned with all his organs gone and head cut off. His mother is obviously traumatized and is uncertain where to go from here, and to be honest, I just don't have answers for her. My heart is breaking, and I feel angry all in one breath. We have had so many children taken from our village in the last couple of months that our team is in shock, and the government is searching for answers and help. Our course is set to expand whether we are ready or not. Prevention is what we are aiming for.
>
> I was outraged and shocked by the murder of this child, and I condemn it in the harshest possible terms. This was a

warning shot from the traffickers. No traffickers bother to return a body; they did it as a warning to the team to stop interfering with their livelihood.

Did it work? Has the team pulled back?

Here's what the Philippines director e-mailed a week after this child was murdered:

> After many setbacks, physical and emotional, being run off the road, and vandalism, we are still standing and focused probably more than even before. Our team members are more determined than even before to protect these children and youth especially. Two weeks ago I was involved in a [trafficking] intervention, which saved several young girls and was an exceptionally rewarding experience. Our most recent test of Born2Fly is going great. The kids are loving it, and the teachers and parent numbers are increasing too. Thank you; blessings and strength to you as you spearhead this movement. We are with you all the way.

What an absolute honor to partner with brave warriors such as this director and her team who are standing up to the despicable actions of these traffickers. Please keep this team in your prayers as they continue to fight on the front lines. They are my heroes.

This war was real. The demons influencing wicked people to commit these atrocities had no regard for human life. What is powerful and poignant, however, is that the people teaching Born2Fly's anti-trafficking program in this city refused to stop. They just kept teaching it. Even more powerful, after losing her child in such a horrific way, this mother said, "My child will not die for nothing. You continue this work." This team's ministry continues to this day.

Hatred for the Wicked

When people hear heinous stories about the terrible things done to children, they often ask me, "Don't you want to physically kill the men who do these terrible things to children, like the guys who butchered this little boy?"

The first time I heard this question, I was surprised. I started thinking about what pimps, child brokers, and pedophiles do to children. My initial reaction was, "Yes, I do want to see these wicked men hurt."

Having brought me to this inner truth about how I felt, God decided it was time for Him to let me know how *He* felt. He revealed to me that the true nature of the God I serve *hates* the abuse happening to the least of these. I knew in my heart that He hates it, and Scripture tells us as much: "You are not a God who takes pleasure in wickedness, nor shall evil dwell with You" (Psalm 5:4).

The Bible also explains *why* God hates sin: "Your iniquities have separated you from your God; and your sins have hidden His face from you, so that He will not hear" (Isaiah 59:2). But the true nature of the God I serve is, most importantly, love—pure, perfect love. Scripture makes this crystal clear to us as well: "He who does not love does not know God, for God is love" (1 John 4:8). God hates sin, but I also know, as difficult as it is to say, that He loves the sinner.

When I began to think about how my human heart desired vengeance for this abuse, it bothered me. I wanted to hold on to my hatred. With every fiber of my being, I wanted to hate the abusers and keep hating the men who buy and sell children like commodities. I wanted to hate the wicked men who have no problem taking money from other wicked men who pay to abuse children. I wanted to hate and keep hating the men who do terrible things to children to satisfy their sick, carnal lusts. I wanted to hate the mothers and fathers who knowingly sell their children to pimps and brothel owners.

But God had a better way for me.

A Gospel That Changes Hearts

These days when people ask if I want to kill the men who do these terrible things to children, I answer with an unequivocal "Yes!" The truth is that I *do* want to see them dead. Every last one of them. Stone dead! I want to see them die *to themselves*. I want each of these men to have the opportunity to hear the gospel, repent, and be reborn in Yeshua.

Please hear me: this doesn't change the fact that perpetrators and abusers need to receive justice for their crimes. I want to see each one arrested, prosecuted, convicted, and jailed for a very long time. Sometimes that's the only way they will consider the brutality of their actions. But as part of their rehabilitation, I also want to see them turn their lives around and live for God.

The man who led me to the first child sex slave I encountered in Cambodia was such a person. I didn't know at first that my guide was a former pimp—that he had actually worked as a child broker and supplied children to pedophiles. It was probably a good thing I was in the dark at the time. Had I known this guy's past from the start, I likely would have felt rather uncomfortable working with him. But this man knew the child sex trade. The night I worked with him, he took me to a place where children as young as four years old were being used for oral sex.

This former pimp had been arrested for his crimes some years ago and had served his time in prison, where he had been saved and had turned his life over to God. His salvation had been so powerful that he had subsequently devoted his life to fighting this horrible crime. Now he worked for a non-governmental organization (NGO) in Cambodia, fighting against the industry he had once championed. Not only does the gospel change the hearts of women and children who have been trafficked, but it also has the power to change the hearts of the traffickers and pedophiles.

It may be hard to stomach (some people get extremely upset with me when I say this), but the truth is that God loves the abuser just as much as the child who's being abused. Scripture makes this clear. He loves the abuser just as much as He loves you and me. He can't *not* love each of us the same, because God *is* love, and He knows each of our lives intimately. His love is not conditional like men's—it's absolutely unconditional. No man or woman, regardless of how bad or evil he or she acts, is beyond redemption:

> You were dead in your trespasses and sins, in which you used to walk when you conformed to the ways of this world and of the ruler of the power of the air, the spirit who is now at work in the sons of disobedience. We all lived among them at one time in the cravings of our flesh, indulging its desires and thoughts. Like the rest, we were by nature children of wrath. But because of His great love for us, God, who is rich in mercy, made us alive with Christ, even when we were dead in our trespasses. It is by grace you have been saved! (Ephesians 2:1–5, BSB)

No one is beyond redemption. Jesus can and will rescue every person who calls on His name. We simply must be obedient and allow Him to work through us. When we do, children will be rescued, and traffickers will be imprisoned and taken off the streets. And maybe, just maybe, if we walk in unconditional love, God will save even the abuser and turn him or her into a powerful weapon against Satan. If this former child broker so steeped in wickedness was able to see the light and accept God's unconditional love and forgiveness, surely there is always hope for others who are blinded by darkness.

Hope kept me going, kept me fighting—in the face of discouragement and evil. Thankfully, we serve a God who knows when we need encouragement and hope that only He can bring at just the right time in just the right way.

14

Anaya

Whoever welcomes one such child in My name welcomes me.
JESUS

Saving a child from a horrific future meant everything to me. James Varghese and his team (Viraj, Dusty, Vikas, and Vaibhav), with whom I had now developed a close working relationship, were a phenomenal asset to the anti-trafficking initiative in India. This team from the Indian Rescue Mission became very adept at putting together operations to rescue unsuspecting underage minors. Anaya is one such child who came to us through James's inspiring initiative.

James had put together a hypothetical scenario for saving underage girls. To employ this operation, Viraj roamed the streets of Mumbai with the team, posing as my representative. I was supposed to be a wealthy businessman coming from America to buy a girl. It wasn't long before Viraj received an offer from someone with a child for sale—a woman selling her younger sister's virginity.

When I received news that James and his team needed upfront money to "hold" the girl's virginity, I immediately became involved in the negotiation process. The sister had asked for two thousand U.S. dollars to keep the girl's virginity intact, but having learned the rules of negotiation, I countered with five hundred. They accepted, so we sent the money to make sure Anaya wouldn't be abused before we could rescue her. She was only twelve years old and living in a quiet village outside of Mumbai.

While our investigative team prepared to rescue Anaya, JOY International paid for the team's food, lodging, and transportation. Along with the upfront money we sent, this operation quickly added up to thousands of dollars. During the planning phase, we also realized we would need to arrange a meeting place so that the police could be present to observe the transaction and catch the predators red handed. The child broker was working with the sister and her husband, who planned to sell the twelve-year-old girl's virginity for seventy thousand rupees—the equivalent of twelve hundred U.S. dollars.

Working closely with the director of the anti-trafficking police in Mumbai, we planned our sting operation. Initially I planned to be the client, but once again, after thinking it through, we realized that if I performed the actual transaction, I would have to travel back and forth to Mumbai as a witness. So we changed the plan. Instead, the scenario would be a wealthy Indian businessman who was looking for a virgin. At that point James stepped in, as he had in Solana's case.

The change naturally created slight confusion, as the team had to explain away the American buyer and exchange him for an Indian buyer. It was a sensitive discussion we had to play carefully. Fortunately, people who traffic other humans for profit usually don't care a great deal about whom they're selling to; they're focused primarily on their profit.

But when we informed them of the different buyer, they told us that they too had a new buyer for the girl, and to simplify the matter they would sell her to him instead. We had no option but to offer more money, which, to our relief, they accepted. This account as well as Solana's rescue, which I shared in chapter 12, highlight how risky these deals are. For all we knew, we might simply be throwing money away. We had to keep hoping, praying, and believing the rescue would happen. I focused on one goal: the child being rescued.

I arrived in Mumbai, and we arranged for James and Viraj to meet the child broker (pimp) in the restaurant of the hotel where I was staying. I positioned myself at a table not far from them while they met. To the average customer, it looked like I was simply typing on my iPad, but in actuality I filmed the entire negotiation process. I was nervous, as usual, because I never knew what would transpire at these exchanges. But more money was handed over, and an arrangement was made to meet the following evening, when they would give us the girl. *So far, so good,* I thought.

Nervous Victory

The next night we went to a McDonald's, as the child broker had requested a public meeting place. Plainclothes police officers lurked outside, waiting for a signal indicating that money had changed hands. Daya Nayak, who directed the local anti-trafficking task force at that time, was a zealous man who despised child abuse and was willing to do whatever it took to rescue a trafficked victim. To be ready for anything and to make sure the perpetrators would by no means escape with the girl, his team had discreetly parked a heavily armored assault vehicle outside. With the child sex trade being a 150 billion-dollar industry, he knew that these people occasionally carried serious firepower.

There's no way out for these evil people, I thought.

Then another thought struck me: *Wait a minute. What if the pimp recognizes me from the night before?* In South Asia I don't exactly blend in, and he could have seen me at the hotel with my iPad. It was way too late in the game, however, to change the plan. I was already in the restaurant. The only bright side was the fact that McDonald's restaurants in Mumbai are always packed. I held my breath and hoped for the best.

When the child broker and the couple walked in with twelve-year-old Anaya, they immediately headed into a different section of the restaurant than where I sat. *Another hitch!* I had to film the transaction. The only thing I could do was wait until they were seated, stand up, and walk into their section, carrying my iPad in its case. I freaked out a little. I couldn't clearly remember pressing "Record," so I wasn't totally sure if the iPad was even recording. The only thing I could do was pray: *God, please let me be recording, and please help me shoot this at the correct angle.* I chose a seat nearby, praying also that the pimp wouldn't recognize me. We serve a God who's in the details.

These deals aren't elaborate affairs; they are simple and swift. The criminals want to minimize their exposure. As soon as the money changed hands, police outside were signaled. Within moments they swarmed in, shouting and ordering the pimp, the sister, and her husband to remain in their seats. In this work we experience rare moments of fulfillment, and that day was fulfilling. All the criminals were arrested, and a female social worker took Anaya into her care.

To maintain an appearance of authenticity to any potential criminals watching the scene, police also arrested our team workers who were involved in the sting. In fact, a policeman who didn't know one of our guys actually punched him square in the face. I suppose this added to the overall legitimacy of the operation, and because the damage wasn't too serious, we found the episode somewhat amusing afterward. Sometimes that's just part of an operation.

Soon after the rescue I nervously checked my iPad, and it had recorded the whole operation. What a relief!

When the social worker questioned a very confused Anaya about the incident, she had no idea about what had actually gone down in the restaurant. Her sister had told her that she would be working as a domestic helper at some wealthy guy's house. Before returning rescue victims home, the police investigate their parents to ensure that they have not been complicit in trafficking their child. If the investigation reveals that the parents have been duped, their child is returned to them. If the investigation team has reason to believe that the parents are complicit, they too are arrested, and the child is sent to a safe house. It turned out that Anaya's parents had been misled by their older daughter, so Anaya was safely returned to them. The sister, her husband, and the pimp were all arrested, prosecuted, and convicted. Each one of them went to prison. Victory!

A Model Operation

This operation had taken into consideration every possible checkpoint to effect a successful rescue and successful prosecutions. We had been fully prepared for any potential difficulties, including having an assault vehicle on standby. It had been a model operation, successfully completed at a cost of just under six thousand dollars.

From a financial perspective, some people might ask if it was worth spending almost six thousand dollars to rescue just one girl. But as I asked earlier, what if it was their child? Then would they ask the question?

If we put a limit on the dollar amount we will spend to rescue one child, are we not then in the same category as those who place a dollar amount to sell a child's body? From a human perspective, it would be worth a hundred or even a thousand times that amount just to rescue one girl.

Even if we look at it financially, the logic holds true. Essentially every operation, even if it's just to save one girl at a time, encompasses more than a single rescue. When we gather enough evidence to put a pimp in prison for many years, we prevent dozens, and likely hundreds or thousands, of women and children from being sold into the sex trade.

In every sense, the money we spent to rescue Anaya was a great investment. Our joy from her rescue was compounded by the knowledge that we had taken three traffickers off the street.

The day Anaya was taken to McDonald's was the first time this quiet young girl had ever set foot in a restaurant. When we asked her if she knew why she was there, she innocently repeated the lie her sister had fed her. Had we not become involved and the sister had managed to sell her to a real pedophile, Anaya's happy life as she knew it would have been over. That night she would have endured an absolute nightmare. Once the wealthy businessman had grown tired of using her after a month or so, he would probably have sold her to a brothel.

When a young girl is no longer desirable—due to having serviced ten to fifteen men a day for several years—especially in Third World countries—the girl is generally sold to a seedier brothel. Once she is owned by these lower-echelon brothels, she is forced to service clientele in a lower-income bracket, which usually means more disease, more violence, and even harsher living conditions than she has already endured. Within a five- to seven-year window, during which the girl is either beaten to death, is infected with AIDS, overdoses on drugs, or chooses to commit suicide, she lives a nightmare.

I thank God that the sting operation for Anaya was a success.

What It Takes for One Rescue in India

The unfortunate reality is that only a handful of organizations in India attempt rescues. A vast amount goes into planning and conducting a rescue, as the following details make clear.

Another rescue operation began several months prior to my arrival in India. I first contacted IRM's James and informed him I would be wiring funds for a rescue operation. I instructed him to begin setting up the initial phase, and he put his team of five in place to start planning for undercover investigations. The wired funds would cover the salaries of IRM's director, the chief investigator (Viraj), and three other field operatives. While the members of this professional team would love to do their work free of charge, they have families to support.

After careful planning, the investigations began. This involved the team going into dance bars and brothels, searching for the youngest girls they could find. Some of the expenses included travel from their home villages to Mumbai, inner-city transportation, food, and lodging. Our teams operate on a frugal budget, choosing lodging options that cost ten to fifteen dollars a night. Their meals are also basic; they eat local cuisine few Westerners would consider palatable. Other expenses include tips for the dance bars (essential during the information-gathering stage) and a few miscellaneous costs. Telephone and communication costs are also necessary, along with the purchase of hidden cameras and surveillance equipment. Team members don't fly between cities; they commute by bus or train, sometimes traveling for twelve hours one way to reach their destination. We focus on being good stewards of the finances donated for rescues. Every dollar saved can go toward rescuing yet another child.

During this particular operation, we incurred an added medical expense when one of our team members was brutally beaten and hospitalized when traffickers discovered he had a hidden camera. Fortunately, he was back at work within two weeks, continuing with undercover investigations. I had dinner with him the night before his return to work to ensure he was back to optimum health. This man's strength of character is admirable. He refuses to be intimidated or deterred.

All these expenses must be met during the planning stages—before even one woman or child is rescued. Once the trafficked victims are rescued, more expenses from medical exams, counselors, and aftercare all come into play. The bottom line is that one rescue operation amounts to thousands of dollars and significant effort. Because I don't take the expensive direct flights, by the time

I finally reached Mumbai for this particular rescue, I had been traveling for more than forty-five hours.

Considering all the expense involved in rescuing children from slavery, it becomes easier to understand why only a handful of organizations are willing to undertake this difficult and dangerous work. At JOY International, we don't just talk about rescuing children and young women. We do whatever it takes to actually go in and rescue sex slaves.

A little-known truth is that many rescue organizations considered to be top echelon advertise their capacity to do rescues but are no longer involved in actual rescues due to the hefty expenses and extreme danger. James and I researched this and could only come up with about four organizations that still do actual rescues on the ground in India—*four* rescue organizations in one country with a population of more than a billion people!

Why so few? Has someone perhaps sat down with a calculator and worked out that all the effort might not be worth the payoff if only one child is rescued? Admittedly, this thought has sometimes flashed through my mind, especially while sitting in airports in Denver, Los Angeles, Bangkok, Tokyo, Seoul, and India. As I watch the hundreds of people walking past, it strikes me that they have no clue that I am on a mission to rescue children forced to be sex slaves in brothels. With 7.6 billion people on Earth, I momentarily wonder if all the months of preparation for each rescue operation, along with the many hours of travel, are really worth it. *Is it really worth the energy and money put into a rescue operation for one solitary child who hardly anyone knows? I don't even know her. I don't know her age. I don't know her name. I don't know what she looks like.*

Of course, I never have to think about it for very long before making up my mind yet again: yes, if only one child is rescued, she is definitely worth it! Following this incontrovertible assertion, a Scripture verse from Luke's Gospel comes to mind: "The very hairs of your head are all numbered. Do not fear therefore; you are of more value than many sparrows" (Luke 12:7).

God created every one of the children we attempt to rescue. He knows each one by name. He knows what she looks like, and He knows the number of hairs on her head. Even as you read this sentence, He also knows where she is and the abuse she's suffering. Children are not created to suffer. Whether it is for one, two, five, ten, or one thousand children, the effort and cost of their rescue is *always* worth it. God loves each child and longs to see each one set free. The book of Psalms gives us a very encouraging, hope-filled scripture: "Those who sow with tears will reap with songs of joy" (Psalm 126:5, NIV).

Your joy is coming, child, I think. *Your joy is coming. Many are going to do what they can to rescue you. God truly loves you, and so do we. You are worth it all.*

But even with wonderful rescues like Solana's and Anaya's, our happiness is often short lived. Within a few days, my heart is grieved again when I'm reminded of how oblivious most of the public is to the realities of this social plague. I wonder if many people simply choose to see no evil, despite the grisly reality standing right in front of them.

Me at five years old
(Kindergarten photo)

SCHOOL LIFE
1957-58

Shirley Temple!

„Ross"   Shirley Temple

Snuggles at the leper colony in Jamshedpur, India, in 1979

Photo by Hal Stack

Snuggles on the streets of Bangladesh in 1979;
this photo was nominated for a Pulitzer Prize.

The slums where the woman washed the mud off my shoes with her hair
in Dhaka, Bangladesh, in 1979

The child I couldn't make smile at Shishu Children's Hospital
in Dhaka, Bangladesh, in 1979

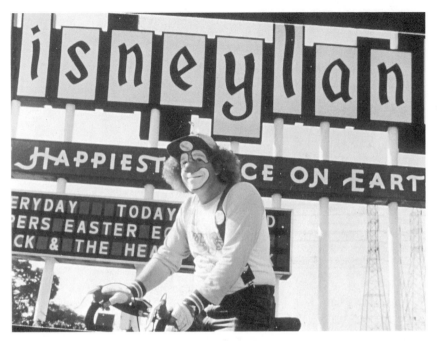

The start of my bike trip across America, April 1, 1981

At Jubilee Pass with my son Lance on our first 101-mile Death Valley walk

Thirteen-year-old girl in a brothel in a Thai village

India Rescue Mission team: James, Vikas, Viraj, me, Vaibhav, and Dusty

Mumbai rescue of twelve-year-old Anaya at a McDonald's;
beside Anaya is her sister, who was selling her, and the pimp

Article detailing Anaya's Mumbai rescue

One of the barefoot children living in the garbage dump
in Phnom Penh, Cambodia, the day I decided to go barefoot

Barefoot boy in Phnom Penh, Cambodia

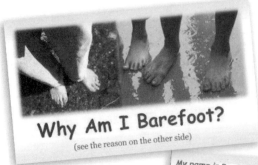

Why Am I Barefoot?

(see the reason on the other side)

My name is Dr. Jeff Brodsky - President of JOY International. We are devoted to the actual rescue of child sex slaves. On July 20th, 2010 I was at a garbage dump in Phnom Phenh, Cambodia. We were looking for children at high risk of being taken by predators and sold to brothels. They were all barefoot. When I went back to my room and took off my shoes, I wondered what it would be like to go through life barefoot every day. I've been barefoot ever since. Going barefoot is my way of showing solidarity with these children and bringing awareness to this atrocity. Please help us fight the worst crime ever perpetrated against an innocent child. Find out how you can help at: WWW.JOY.ORG

The front and back of my "Why Am I Barefoot?" card

Me with Kelly Treat, whose group hosted the first Barefoot Mile in Coshocton, Ohio

SWAT team members on Barefoot Mile, Anchorage, Alaska, May 2017

Alaska Barefoot Mile: me, Gwen Adams (Priceless director), Alaska first lady Donna Walker, Senator Lisa Murkowski, Anchorage mayor Ethan Berkowitz, Josh Pepperd (sponsor and owner of Davis Constructors)

Me with my heroes Don and Bridget Brewster, founders of AIM (Agape International Missions), in Svay Pak, Cambodia

Hannah Porter on a missions trip to Cambodia giving away rice; twenty years earlier we walked 101 miles across Death Valley to raise funds for her adoption.

The child-killing tree at the Killing Fields outside Phnom Penh, Cambodia

Fifth anniversary Barefoot Mile in Phnom Penh, Cambodia;
what a joy to see Cambodian nationals bringing life to their country!

A rescue operation in Phnom Penh, Cambodia, carried out with the Anti-Human Trafficking Juvenile Protection Police and the AIM SWAT team

Another rescue operation in Phnom Penh

Robert training the Anti-Human Trafficking Juvenile Protection Police and AIM SWAT team, October 2017

Graduation for the Anti-Human Trafficking Juvenile Protection Police and AIM SWAT team, March 2018

Me with General Pol Pithei of the Anti-Human Trafficking
Juvenile Protection Police, March 2018

Twelve-year-old Gracelyn presenting me with the money she earned for JOY International making and selling bracelets

Izac Shirley, my then twelve-year-old grandson, with his prize-winning pig, Mr. Wiggles; Izac donated part of his prize money to JOY International.

Gail and me

PART 3

SOLIDARITY
WITH
THE
LEAST

15

Going Barefoot

*No man is worth his salt who is not ready at all times to
risk his well-being, to risk his body, to risk his life, in a great cause.*
THEODORE ROOSEVELT

July 19, 2010, marked another turning point in my life and ministry.

My friend Jim Rogers and I had gone to the city garbage dump in Phnom Penh to help with a feeding program. We stood watching as local children ate a lunch of chicken and rice. A few of them walked around in old, torn flip-flops, but a dozen or so sat on the side of the clearing. They were all barefoot—visual reminders of their vulnerability.

Through my travels and work fighting child trafficking, I've learned that throughout the world public garbage dumps are breeding grounds for sexual predators. Many children who grow up in or near these places are at extremely high risk of being kidnapped and sold into brothels to work as sex slaves.

That night, as I unlaced my Rockports back in my hotel, the image of those barefoot children flashed across my eyes. I sat on the edge of my bed looking at my strong, comfortable shoes, and a strange thought came to me: *I wonder what it would be like to have to go barefoot every day?*

After a lengthy discussion with God, I came to a decision. I had no idea what a major impact this decision would have, nor did I suspect the changes it would bring to the rest of my life. I immediately took off my shoes and socks, placed my socks inside the shoes, and packed the shoes with the socks inside into my small suitcase, feeling surprisingly great about this new resolve.

During dinner with Jim (yes, I was barefoot), I told him about my decision.

"I'm either going barefoot or wearing sandals for one whole year," I explained.

Within a few months, I had made up my mind not to wear even sandals and instead to go totally barefoot for an entire year.

When I flew home and met my wife at the Denver airport, Gail looked at my bare feet in wonderment.

"I've decided to go barefoot for a year," I told her.

"What do you mean, you're going barefoot?" asked Gail. "Jeff, you don't live in a warm-weather climate; you happen to live in the mountains of Colorado!"

We actually live at an elevation of 8,900 feet.

"What are you going to do in the winter?" An edge of consternation crept into her voice.

"I'm gonna get cold feet," I said, expecting her to laugh. She didn't.

"Seriously, Jeff. What are you going to do in the winter? What about when it snows?"

"I'm gonna get cold feet!"

I didn't know how else to respond. I went into more detail.

"Gail, I *have* to do this. God has called me to go barefoot for a year in solidarity with the children I saw and millions of other impoverished children around the world who are at high risk of being forced into the child sex trade. I have to do this to bring awareness to more people on their behalf. No matter how bad the weather may be, I will be barefoot. I made a decision that I will not compromise. I really don't want to suffer frostbite, Gail, so I promise, I will be extremely careful. But please understand, I have to do this."

To say that God has blessed me with a remarkably loving woman would be an outrageous understatement. When God introduced me to Gail, He knew the things He would call me to do, and He knew the kind of woman I would need as my partner in life, love, and calling. I couldn't have been as successful as I have been without Gail at my side. I truly thank God for her every day. In more than forty years of marriage, not one day has passed that I haven't told her, "I love you."

Gail has truly been a partner with me on this barefoot journey that started in 2010. The first time it snowed, I soon realized that walking barefoot was extremely painful and treacherous. I learned quickly that I had to know my limitations—what my skin could endure before frostbite set in. I also discovered other, less obvious perils. For example, when leaving the warm interior of a building, the outdoor humidity and temperature could cause my skin to freeze in seconds. I rapidly came to the conclusion that this barefoot business was not for sissies!

After seeing how the first flurry of snow affected me, Gail shoveled a path from our front door to the car (about twenty-five feet) every time it snowed. When the path was cleared, she started the car engine and turned on the heater to warm up the car for me. She also placed a towel on the floorboard so I could dry my feet. I told her she didn't have to do these things, but she ignored my protests. The depth of Gail's love and care for me knows no bounds. I am truly overwhelmed by my wife's love.

In Public

Those early days, weeks, and months of being barefoot in public were quite challenging for me, especially when I went into restaurants and supermarkets. I was confronted all the time. The situation became so problematic that I began investigating online what the legal standing was for being barefoot in public, especially in the United States. I soon found helpful organizations like the Society for Barefoot Living (also known as SBL, barefooters.org), which has a few thousand members from all over the world. I also found the Barefoot Alliance (barefootalliance.org). These organizations' websites had a myriad of information that was a huge help to me. What I learned from them was good news.

The simple fact is that there is not one state in America in which legally a person *must* wear shoes in a restaurant or grocery store (or any retail establishment, for that matter)—no prohibitive laws, no health-code violations. What many people perceive to be a violation of law is just not the case. Walking barefoot in public establishments is not against the law. It's a misconception many people have, perhaps due to signs like "No Shoes, No Shirt, No Service." I actually have letters from the health departments of every state in America proving that it's not a legal violation to appear barefoot in any public place. Now each establishment, of course, *does* have the right to enforce its own dress-code rules. On these grounds it may insist on shoes, but this right is not based on any health code.

Surprisingly, even when I have explained to people in detail that our American legal system has no problem with people being barefoot in public, it has made no difference in how some of them have treated me. Many have preconceived notions of how civil people dress, and if I haven't fit in with their notions, they have, sometimes belligerently, made me aware of their opinions. At times that has been quite disheartening.

When you think about it, it makes sense why there's no legal violation for walking barefoot. There is clearly no difference between the dirt under my feet and the dirt under someone's shoes. In fact, I'm pretty certain that what clings to the soles of people's shoes is much worse than what can be found under my feet on any given day.

It's a simple exercise in logic. When people wearing shoes walk in public streets, they generally look straight ahead, giving little thought to what they have stepped on. This is certainly not the case when I walk a public street! *No way!* I have learned the art of walking barefoot. First, I always look down. I want to know exactly what I'll be stepping on—broken glass, a nail, a cigarette, spit (a lot of people spit, especially in India), dog feces. Who knows what! To avoid these many "obstacles," I walk with my eyes on my feet.

At the end of the day, without fail the second thing I do after I come home (kissing Gail is first) is go directly into the bathroom. I sit on the edge of the tub, swing my feet into it, run hot water, soak my feet, coat my loofah with scented anti-bacterial soap, and scrub my feet until they're clean. Every day.

When you get home from being out all day, do you remove your shoes? Maybe. But more than likely you just walk into your house. If so, you're tracking in everything you stepped on throughout the day. All those germs (and who knows what else) are still under your shoes. How many people take their shoes off every day and scrub the soles with anti-bacterial soap? All the germs growing and festering under those shoes are still there, being tracked into people's homes. As I said, on any given day, the soles of my feet are likely to be cleaner than the soles of people's shoes!

Why Am I Barefoot?

During those first months, I was asked so many times why I was barefoot that I actually had a card printed to explain it. One side portrays a picture of my bare feet alongside the bare feet of those very children in Cambodia who motivated me to go barefoot in the first place. Underneath the picture in large words is the caption "Why Am I Barefoot? (see the reason on the other side)."

The back of the card carries this message:

My name is Dr. Jeff Brodsky—President of JOY International. We are devoted to the actual rescue of child sex slaves. On July 20th, 2010, I was at a garbage dump in Phnom

Penh, Cambodia. We were looking for children at high risk
of being taken by predators and sold to brothels. They were
all barefoot. When I went back to my room and took off
my shoes, I wondered what it would be like to go through
life barefoot every day. I've been barefoot ever since. Going
barefoot is my way of showing solidarity with these children and bringing awareness to this atrocity. Please help us
fight the worst crime ever perpetrated against an innocent
child. Find out how you can help at: www.joy.org.

I have handed out these cards all over the world, and each
time I'm astounded at how the majority of people completely shift
their perception. The response has truly been wonderful—most of
the time. Once in a while, a person is rude. A few are even mean
and hurtful.

In my years of walking about barefoot, I have been thrown
out of only one store. The manager of a national superstore in
Littleton, Colorado, didn't care about my reason for being barefoot
or the letter from the Colorado Health Department I presented
to him. He stubbornly insisted that I either put on shoes or leave.
He even had two security guards physically escort me to the exit.

A little annoyed by how stubborn he was, I asked him to show
me a copy of the store policy. Of course there wasn't one. He then
threatened to call the police. If Gail hadn't been with me, I would
have encouraged him to follow through, but it seemed unfair to
put my wife through something so traumatic. After hearing my
story, a lawyer I knew wanted to sue the store for discrimination,
but instead of pursuing tedious legal recourse, I decided to let
sleeping dogs lie.

Another time I was at a Veterans of Foreign Wars breakfast.
Seeing a friend, I went over to say hello. My friend was sitting with
a man I recognized from a local church. I put my hand out to greet
him, but his response shocked me.

"Back off!" he shouted.

"Excuse me?" I asked, not sure I had heard him correctly. "Is something wrong?"

"I don't care for what you're doing with your bare feet. Now back off, and get away from me!"

To worldly people who don't know any better, this kind of behavior from a Christian gives all Christians a bad name—a person's actions can seldom be separated from who they really are, despite how they label themselves. I walked away in shock and in tears.

Typically, upon entering a restaurant, a hostess or a manager usually confronts me, and the conversation goes something like this:

"Sir, do you have shoes?"

"No, I don't."

"You need to wear shoes in here."

"Really, why?"

"Because entering barefoot is a health-code violation. It's the law."

This is where I ask the critical question: "Is that the only reason?"

"Yes."

"Well, then we're fine," I explain, "because I have a letter from the director of the Health Department for the state of Colorado [or whichever state I happen to be in at the time] that clearly states that there is no health-code violation or any law or regulation about being barefoot or having to wear shoes in a restaurant."

Following this, I take out the letter and show it to the person. Often he or she is genuinely thankful for the information and even asks to copy the letter.

When I give my permission to copy the letter, I usually hand the person a copy of my barefoot card, and then I'm cordially seated. Often when the individual returns my letter, the person expresses how deeply he or she has been moved by my reason for going barefoot.

Keep Going!

That year passed slowly. Each month brought me closer to my deadline—the day I could wear my socks and shoes again.

The day finally came. When I woke up on July 19, 2011, I was beyond excited. Few things had ever felt so good to the touch as the white cotton socks in my hand that morning. I couldn't wait to feel their warmth and softness covering my bare feet. I sat down on the couch, stretched the first sock a little, and eagerly brought it toward my left foot. But as hard as I tugged, I couldn't pull the sock past my toes.

What on earth? With a little more determination, I tried again to pull the sock over my foot. But again, it didn't move. It was as if someone (an angel?) were there, pulling the sock in the other direction—away from my foot. *This is crazy*, I thought. But over the years, I've learned that when something unexplainable is happening, it's usually God. I cried out, "Lord, I don't understand what's happening. What else do You want from me? I just went an entire year barefoot!"

The words He immediately impressed upon my heart were straightforward and simple: "Keep going! Those children are still out there."

Soon I was on the floor weeping, overwhelmed by the power of God's presence.

Suddenly, it was as if I was back in Phnom Penh witnessing the same scenes that had started all this a year earlier on July 19, 2010. I saw the bare feet of the children I had watched that day as they ran around the disease-infested garbage dump. That image of those children with no shoes had wrecked me and started me on a path I never would have imagined traveling.

I wept uncontrollably. The Lord reminded me of those barefoot children who were at such high risk of being snatched by traffickers and forced to become sex slaves—the horrific life no child should ever be exposed to.

I put down my socks and had a serious conversation with God as I reflected on the past year. I thought of how many people had commented on my bare feet, especially during the icy winters in Colorado. I recalled the articles written about me being barefoot and the scores of people who had contacted me after they heard about the why behind my story. Many were thrilled to be involved and had even helped in rescues. I realized that my choice to live barefoot had given voice to the cause.

When Gail woke up and came downstairs, she noticed that I was still barefoot.

"Jeff, I thought for sure you would be wearing socks!"

"I have decided to keep going barefoot," I said.

Slightly shocked, she asked the obvious question: "Why?" Then she asked how long I intended to keep doing this. She listened as I explained in concrete terms that day or night, rain, sun, or snow, I had decided to live barefoot indefinitely.

"During the past year, being barefoot has helped me share the plight of the children we're trying to reach. Seeing my bare feet has given people an opportunity to respond, allowing me to educate them about trafficked children. Some have even responded financially, helping fund our rescues."

I held my wife's hand and looked into her eyes. "Gail, by staying barefoot, if I can motivate even one person a year to action or to help us rescue just one more child, I'll go barefoot the rest of my life."

She knew I was serious.

The strange thing is, I hate being barefoot. When I'm asked why I'm barefoot, I always respond, "One word: obedience. I'm being obedient to what I believe God has asked me to do."

What I had thought would be the end of my challenge was only the beginning. God wasn't done. Something as simple as putting on a pair of socks became my crossroads.

16

In Our Own Backyard

Knowing what's right doesn't mean much unless you do what's right.
FRANKLIN ROOSEVELT

Several years ago, one of my friends resigned as pastor of a church in Ohio to accept an associate pastor position at a large church in Texas. After he settled into his new job, I e-mailed him, expressing my congratulations. I told him I would love to visit to share with his new congregation the work JOY International is doing. He checked with the rest of the pastoral team, but sadly, they decided against my visit. Apparently they were concerned that my message might offend and even scare some members of their congregation.

Are you kidding? I thought. I knew with certainty that large churches were at risk from sexual predators who focused on their youth groups. In fact, church youth groups were one of the prime targets these pimp predators honed in on, looking for young girls to recruit. It was happening in churches all around the world but especially in America.

The U.S. State Department's 2017 Trafficking in Persons report breaks out each country into one of three tiers according to the individual country's efforts to combat human trafficking. The United States is on tier one, indicating that our nation fully meets the minimum standards of the Trafficking Victims Protection Act of 2000 for the elimination of trafficking; still, the minimum standards may not be enough.[1] The United States has definite trafficking problems, and those problems are increasing. According to a recent study funded by the Department of Justice, the average age of young girls forced into the sex trade in America is approximately sixteen years old.[2] Though estimates vary, as many as 21,000 child sex slaves, or children who are trafficked, may exist *just in America*.[3]

For many years I was an American youth pastor, so I had experience recognizing these young targets. Within thirty seconds of observing a new youth at my meetings, I could usually tell if he or she wanted to be there or if the parents or guardians had forced the young person to go. When we entered into praise and worship, my first impression was generally validated. The young people who weren't there by choice stayed seated, looking bored, or maybe they stood beside the other teens but just went through the motions.

Girls who displayed this disinterested attitude fit the profile predators quickly targeted. Pimps were looking to recruit these girls. The predators knew that youth groups were soft targets because they often included the kind of girl who fit the profile they sought.

I was not trying to instill fear in seeking to speak to churches, but I was not exaggerating the real potential for threat. I could point to specific sources, including videos, that verified this abuse—young girls targeted by their so-called boyfriends whom they had met in a youth group. I came to call these men who seduced young girls into a life of prostitution "loverboys." Increasingly, anti-trafficking groups were using the same term.

Loverboys

Essentially, loverboys are pimps. Either they're full-fledged pimps doing business for themselves, or they're young men whom pimps recruit and train to ultimately fulfill this role. They are sometimes teenagers or guys in their early twenties and are usually good-looking. They target young females, purposely placing themselves in strategic positions to make easy acquaintances with the full intention of causing these young girls to develop romantic interests in them. Once a relationship has developed, their main goal is to force the girls into prostitution. This makes it clear that these girls aren't "prostitutes"; they are *prostituted* for the profit of others.

This kind of manipulation is not only happening in some far-flung region of the world. It's happening every day in America everywhere—the inner city, the suburbs, rural towns, and city centers.

While it can be shocking to hear that these loverboy pimps or pimps in training are operating here in America, even more shocking is how blatantly they're doing it. I won't list any of the titles of the books being sold online (I refuse to give Satan any glory), but check out this blurb on the inside cover of one pimp-training manual sold on Amazon: "Everything that a person wonders about pimping but was ashamed or afraid to ask; without a doubt the best and most comprehensive book ever published on The Game."

"The Game" is a reference to pimping, also known as "mackin'." It's literally a sport of seduction. More than twenty of this type of book are available online, offering complete step-by-step guides to the art of becoming a pimp at the click of a button. I'm not talking about young men just manipulating girls to sleep with them. These books are about seducing young women into *forced prostitution*. They offer detailed information on how to charge and receive payment and how a pimp goes in pursuit of finding a young girl to prostitute. They even go as far as breaking down the fundamentals of turning a "fresh" prostitute out into the "game."

How did we manage to go so wrong?

The Love Factor

How does recruiting from youth groups work?

Some young stud decides to read one of these pimp-training books. Once he has learned the basic strategy, he realizes that plenty of girls attend local youth-group meetings, so he joins a group to see if he can attract some girls.

Visibly disconnected girls are prime targets. They're easily distracted from the leader's message, especially if they see a handsome young man to focus on. The loverboy, meanwhile, starts working his angles, making inroads on becoming "the boyfriend." He'll wine and dine a girl, pulling out all the stops, as he does everything he can to ensure that she thinks he's sincere and charming. After all, she's going to earn him a ton of money. All his initial effort will be worth it later.

In America a pretty young woman can earn a pimp between five thousand and twenty-five thousand dollars *a month*. One girl can earn her pimp a salary between fifty thousand and two hundred fifty thousand a year—just one girl. Those pimps who work a stable of six or seven girls can become millionaires. And it's easy money once the girl has serviced her first client.

But how, you may be thinking, *do they manage to convince a girl to be prostituted?*

Through JOY International's work in the United States, we've uncovered numerous stories that usually go something like this.

Having assured the girl of his love and devotion, suddenly one night the loverboy becomes really emotional.

"Suzy, I'm in a lot of trouble; hon, I don't know what to do."

"What do you mean?" (Remember, she's already in love with this sleazeball and has been for some time.)

"Well, I owe these guys a lot of money."

"What do you mean? What kind of money?"

"I owe several thousand dollars to this group of men, and if I don't give it to them, they're going to kill me."

"Kill you!" she gasps in horror.

"Yeah," he replies mournfully.

At this point he's trying to gain control of her mind. Once he owns her mind, he controls her whole body. Then he can manipulate her into doing whatever he wants her to do.

"These guys," he continues, "you've already met them. They think you're really hot. I don't blame them for saying so, because you really are! I was pretty shocked, but one of them actually said to me, 'Listen, if you let me have sex with your lady, I'll knock a thousand dollars off the money you owe me.'"

Of course it's all a ploy. He doesn't owe anybody a thing. The guy who's going to have sex with her will be paying the pimp—her supposed boyfriend—to use her for sex. The loverboy tricks her into thinking she'll be canceling some of his debt by having sex with this guy.

Sex starts with one guy, then goes on to the next guy, with each incident ending in him telling her how grateful he is and how much he loves her for saving him from these thugs. At some point he casually suggests to her that this is actually easy money, and if she doesn't mind, she could rid him of his debt altogether! Then they could start saving for marriage or a trip to Mexico or Disneyland. He subtly finds out what makes her happy and then "helps" her see how she can make her dreams come true just by having sex with a few guys.

The Danger Is Real

I was disappointed to be denied an opportunity to share this vital message with my friend's new church. As JOY International expanded, I was continually amazed at pastors who reacted to the epidemic of sex trafficking this way. I might *offend* their congregation? What happened to *protecting* them? What if one of those girls in their youth group was recruited and forced into the sex trade? Suddenly it would be too late! Unable to accept my friend's refusal without first making sure his pastoral staff understood my message, I said to him, "Wait a minute, aren't pastors supposed to protect their sheep from wolves? The wolves are coming into our churches because our leadership is turning a blind eye."

They wouldn't budge.

Let's be honest. Often church leaders don't want to make the hard decisions to avoid offending people because if church members take offense, they might simply look for another church to attend. Perhaps parents fear that if their children hear this message, they will ask questions that the parents are not prepared to answer. Or maybe leaders have to make a choice: do they protect the people under their care, or do they protect the tithes and offerings these people give? It may seem pathetic that church leaders would even contemplate such a choice, but unfortunately I see it happen far too often.

Surely the warning given to the "overseers" of the "flock" in the book of Acts is a pertinent analogy in this instance. Those who "shepherd the church of God" are specifically warned about "savage wolves" that "will come in among [the church], not sparing the flock" (Acts 20:28–29). Knowing this danger firsthand and recognizing the potential signs as they unfold, I feel a sense of responsibility to warn the body of Christ about this very real danger. Too many church leaders deny their members an opportunity to receive a word of warning and in doing so limit their scope of protection.

17

A Lucrative Trade

The truth is sometimes worse than what you might imagine.
NITA BELLES

Not all American girls are lured into sex slavery by deception. Another grim scenario leverages the fear factor rather than the love factor. While the loverboy scheme is probably the most common ploy used to gain control over a girl, in drastic situations these guys resort to fear mongering. They will do whatever it takes to force a girl to earn money for them.

Nor are all girls trafficked from church, of course. They are targeted at school, in malls, at parties. There are even numerous stories about girls being trafficked right out of their homes. Holly Austin Smith is just one example of a young woman who was trafficked this way. She wrote a powerful book called *Walking Prey: How America's Youth Are Vulnerable to Sex Slavery*. Theresa Flores, author of *The Slave Across the Street*, wrote about her experience of being trafficked while living at home in middle America.

Sex trafficking in the United States is beyond the ghettos and inner cities. Loverboys and fear-mongering pimps have no respect for social status. Rich or poor, it doesn't matter. All that matters is being able to manipulate a girl into having sex to make them money.

The Fear Factor

The moneyman (or pimp) starts the ball rolling by approaching some young guy. Here's how it plays out.

"You want to make some extra money?" the pimp asks the guy.

"Yeah, what do I have to do?"

"Listen carefully, and you can make an extra thousand dollars!"

"A thousand dollars? What do I have to do? I'm not going to kill anybody."

"No, I don't want you to kill anybody. Are you capable of finding yourself a girlfriend?"

"Yeah, of course I can find a girlfriend. Yeah, that's easy."

The moneyman plays on the young guy's virility, questioning whether he can really attract a girl to go out with him. He challenges his manhood.

"Okay, go get yourself a girlfriend, but don't fall in love with her. You're just going to get her to do what I need her to do. You're going to bring her to me, and then you're done with her, and I'll give you a thousand dollars. Then you go and find someone else, and I'll give you another thousand dollars." Or five hundred dollars, or whatever price the guy is willing to settle for.

Because this pimp probably already has a bevy of girls in his stable, he has the resources to give the loverboy an iPhone to use.

"I want you to text me with all the useful information you can access. Send details about her family. I want to know who her brother is, her mother, her sister, her father. Find out where they go to school or where they work. Gather all the information you can, and send it to me. When I'm satisfied with what you've sent, I'll have you invite the girl to a party."

So the loverboy goes out and finds a girlfriend, accesses all the personal information the moneyman needs, and sends it to him. Then the moneyman says, "Bring her to this address; tell her it's a party or whatever." Finally the unsuspecting girl arrives. The moneyman meets her, and her life will never be the same again. He takes her hand and says, "Hey, Sarah, do you know who I am? I'm your new daddy!"

"Excuse me?" she pulls her hand away. He just laughs.

"Yeah," he says, "I'm your new daddy!" The first spark of fear in her eyes amuses him. "You're going to respect your new daddy, because from now on, everything you get is going to be from me. You're going to do whatever I tell you to do. If I tell you to have sex with five or six guys a day, you're going to do it."

"I would never do that! You're crazy." The fear has edged into her voice now, and she's eyeing the door.

"Oh yes, you definitely *will* do whatever I tell you! Let me show you why you're going to listen to your daddy."

He picks up a remote control for the big flat-screen TV mounted to the wall and pushes a button. Boom! Up pops a picture of her little brother, Timmy. "Hey, look at this! It's your kid brother, Timmy. I believe he's quite a hit with the little girls in his school. Doesn't he go to the middle school right here in town?"

"Yeah, he does," she confirms in shock. Her voice is so soft she can barely be heard. But he doesn't need an answer.

"Well, sweetheart, if you don't do what we tell you, Timmy's dead! We're going to kill him." He lets this sink in. He has her full attention now.

He brings up another image. "See your sister, Hayley? Now you don't do what we tell you, Hayley's also dead. But we'll take our time with her. I'll make sure my boys have some fun before they kill her. Oh, and look what we have here," he says animatedly, flicking through pictures of an attractive older woman. "Look at that! Who is this beauty? That's your mom, right? She works down at the electric company, and we even know the route she takes to work."

He puts his finger under Sarah's chin and raises her face until she is looking into his eyes. "Now if you don't do what we tell you, your momma? She's dead! Your dad, he's dead too! Your new daddy is gonna kill them. Now if you want your family dead, that's cool with me. No problem. Just don't do what we tell you. But if you do want them to live, you'll do *whatever* we tell you to do. Every time! You understand me now, sugar?"

These wicked men instill fear into the girl's mind so they can control her. They start out by using fear, but if she's still not compliant, they employ other techniques to gain control. They may drug her, undress her, and gang rape her while filming the entire sordid episode. Later they'll show her the video and tell her, "If you don't do what we tell you to do, we'll send this video to all your friends and your entire family. We'll post it online, and everybody will see what kind of girl you are—what kinds of things you do in your leisure time."

Once they gain control of a girl, when she has become just another statistic in the game—what pimps refer to as "the life"—she begins to believe that there is no turning back. She believes that this is who she is now and this is what she must do to keep her family safe. She loses all hope of ever leading a normal life again.

Organized Crime

American gangs are now starting to realize that human trafficking is an extremely lucrative trade. They have figured out that pimping these young girls is far more rewarding than drugs.

If I'm a drug dealer, I first have to purchase a quantity of marijuana, amphetamines, heroin, or whatever substance I deal in. Then I have to find my customer and sell him an ounce of my poison. I mark up the product, sell it to him or her once, and then I need to procure more product. I can only sell the drug *once*.

But a fifteen-year-old girl can be sold numerous times every day most days of the year. She can be sold once every hour for several hours a day, or even once every fifteen minutes if guys are looking for a quickie. Some girls have shared horror stories about being forced to service more than twenty men a day. *Seven days a week.* Suddenly, the "merchandise" becomes highly valuable because the pimp doesn't have to outlay any money to replenish his stock.

The holidays Americans cherish so dearly are an absolute nightmare for prostituted girls. Holidays mean a large percentage of the male population has the day off work. These guys have extra time on their hands, so they want to go and grab a girl. A national holiday means she must work twice as hard to keep all those additional customers happy.

Gangs and organized crime have realized that putting girls into the sex trade is a much better return on their investment, and they can make more money with girls than they can with drugs.

Sadly, the FBI states that once caught in this web, the average remaining lifespan of these girls ranges from five to seven years.[1] They'll die of disease, commit suicide, or even fall prey to murder.

If this doesn't break your heart, make sure it's beating.

18

After a Rescue

The ache for home lives inside all of us,
the safe place where we can come as we are.

MAYA ANGELOU

When a major sting operation took place throughout America in 2015, with multiple FBI and anti-trafficking units across the country working together for more than a year on this lone operation, comments flooded my Facebook page. Most of the messages resonated with the same basic idea: "This is a major blow to child trafficking!"

When the various teams finally went into action during the final stage of the operation, 149 young people were rescued.[1] Many were underage, the majority of them teenagers. I was really blessed by the fact that the authorities perceived the operation as a rescue. It was refreshing to know that *rescue* had been their focus.

As overjoyed as I was to know that these young people were now safe, I couldn't help thinking about the hundreds of thousands of children who still need to be rescued. Let's break down the numbers. As mentioned in chapter 16, in the United States alone, as many as 21,000 children may be trafficked. In this operation 149 were rescued, which means the rescue percentage of this operation equals a little more than half of 1 percent of trafficked children in the United States. Sadly, I can't call that a "major blow to child trafficking."

I have to ask, what are we doing about the 21,000 children who still need to be rescued? This has to be our focus now. But not only that—where will these 149 rescued children go? What follow-up work will be done for them? A rescue is a wonderful thing, but the children who are rescued need a great deal of specialized care after the horror they have endured. Sadly, in America we have very few resources to address this need.

Specific and Special Needs

Currently the United States has only a few hundred beds in the entire nation specifically for children who are rescued from the child sex trade. These children have specific needs following the trauma of being trafficked and continually raped multiple times a day. Sexually abused children shouldn't be placed in the same homes or detention centers designated for generally troubled youngsters, which is usually where they wind up. They shouldn't be put into the same home as juvenile delinquents, drug addicts, or children caught stealing. These abused children require a special facility and a specific methodology. They are *victims*, and following their rescue, they need their dignity and self-worth restored.

They need to be gently reintegrated into society and allowed to find a safe space within a community where they will be valued for their intrinsic humanity, not just for their youth or good looks. Finally, they need the right tools to prevent them from being drawn back into the life from which they've been rescued. All this takes the limitless love and patience of professionally trained counselors, and that carries a huge financial cost.

These specific needs have caused me to value the professional relationship I have developed with Dr. Kalyani Gopal, an Indiana-based clinical psychologist of the highest caliber. Her main focus is to ensure that rescued girls are placed in the proper facility and receive the necessary restorative care.

Four Elements of Rescue

The work of JOY International involves four major practical elements.

First, *rescue*. This is our primary goal. When we learn that a girl is being used as a sex slave in a brothel, we do whatever it takes to free her from captivity (which includes my walking barefoot since 2010!).

Second is *restoration*. Six elements are vital to the process of a girl's restoration in a safe house, also referred to as a restoration home. If all six criteria are not met, a high percentage of the girls in the program will return to the sex trade, because it's all they know. If all six elements *are* met, we've found that a large percentage will go on to lead productive lives. The six criteria of restoration include healing on these levels:

1. Physical
2. Emotional
3. Psychological
4. Educational
5. Spiritual
6. Vocational

Vocational restoration is dependent on the age of the person being restored. Providing a good education for a ten-year-old is more important than focusing on her vocational training. A woman who's twenty-eight years old, however, needs to focus on a vocation rather than a traditional education. So vocation is age dependent, but all six elements are crucial to the restoration process at various stages in the victim's life.

Third, *reintegration*. Reintegrating abused girls back into society is another critical step toward their long-term wellbeing. Regardless of which country they're in, giving them the opportunity to become productive citizens allows them to finally start leading a normal life.

In Cambodia I had the opportunity of visiting the home of Danni, a girl who was rescued from extremely dire straits. It was fascinating to see the end result of her rescue, restoration, and reintegration process, especially when reuniting with her family, who were all so joyful in their reunion with her. Witnessing firsthand how a child has been reintegrated into society and thus become a productive citizen is perhaps the most enjoyable part of my job.

Danni was taught a trade as part of her restoration and reintegration process. She is now a seamstress in her village and runs a successful business.

In the West, if you want to buy an outfit for your daughter, you go to a mall or store, try on clothes, and then buy the outfit. Cambodian villages have no malls, cars, or money, for that matter. How does a family living in these conditions buy clothing? They visit a local seamstress. If they have no money to spend, they implement the age-old practice of bartering. They might trade a bag of rice, a chicken, two dozen eggs, a gallon of goat's milk, or a few pounds of goat meat. In this way Danni became a real blessing to her community, and especially to her family.

Rescued from a brothel, she went through the healing process, which started with ensuring that she was physically healthy. Then counseling helped her process her emotional wounds and work through the psychological trauma she had experienced. Having received healing in these areas, Danni was able to receive spiritual renewal. Finally, she was taught to be a seamstress, a trade in which she showed interest. Danni has no electricity in her house, so her electric sewing machine runs on a car battery. But she makes it work, and she makes it work well. We in the prosperous West can learn so much from people who lead simple lives. Her newfound life is the epitome of what JOY International aims to accomplish with every person we rescue.

Finally, *prevention*. JOY International helps prevent human trafficking, especially child trafficking, in a number of ways—educating children and parents about the ploys of traffickers; stemming poverty through food, clothing, and shoe distribution; supporting safe houses for at-risk children to hear the gospel and receive love; and sending short-term teams to minister in various countries.

Awareness is also an important aspect of prevention. Making parents aware of trafficking is the first step through which they're empowered to protect themselves and their children.

Another aspect of prevention is special training for the local armed forces. I have helped with the education of special forces in Brazil and also worked alongside a former detective from the United Kingdom. JOY International has even provided the funds for a general in the Cambodian police's anti-human trafficking task force to finance successful rescue operations (see chapter 25). For this we work with Agape International Mission (AIM). This special forces program is working wonders in the field. Unfortunately, the training regular police officers receive isn't specialized. The men of this anti-trafficking task force need education, expert field training, additional pay, and superior weaponry. That's where JOY International and ministries like AIM come in.

Arresting a perpetrator, however, is the greatest form of prevention. Every perpetrator arrested could ultimately prevent hundreds, if not thousands, from being trafficked and abused.

A Safe Village

JOY International is also involved in a partnership with Dr. Gopal for developing a safe village in the Unites States for rescued underage children.

I dream of seeing rescued girls befriending each other, running and jumping together, creating arts and crafts, and getting the counseling they need to heal in a safe place, immersed in natural beauty. Is there any sound more beautiful than the laughter of an innocent child? I want to see their pain healed—to see a twinkle in their eyes, sparkling again as they finally realize that their nightmare is over. I want to see beauty for ashes, sorrow turned to joy. And I want to hear the sound of their laughter ringing out to heaven against a clear blue sky—to see each child grow and mature, to be given the opportunity to become all God created her to be.

Ultimately, my end goal is to see these girls come to know their Creator and the God who rescued and will restore them. I want them to know that God is glorified by their individual rescues. Although men and women may have planned the physical details of their rescues, it is God who ultimately orchestrated and has overseen them.

Whenever we rescue a girl, our hope is that she understands a few vital truths after being set free:

> God did not forget about you. God is not the one who abused you. He motivated the right people, who then arranged to set you free. God loves you. He didn't want those terrible things to happen to you. The people you saw being led away in handcuffs are the ones who wanted that to happen to you. The men who abused you, they wanted it to happen to you. Now they're in prison, and you are free. It was God who arranged for you to be set free.

One Nepalese girl, who was drugged and trafficked across the border into a brothel in India, was the feature of a documentary titled *The Day My God Died*.[2] During her captivity in a brothel, she felt as if God had deserted her. She wondered how He could have allowed such a terrible thing to happen. Thankfully, she was rescued, and her faith in God was restored. But many are less fortunate. They spend their lives enslaved in the sex trade.

The facility JOY International is raising funds for in the U.S. will eventually accommodate more than one hundred girls. However, considering the scale of the problem and the shortage of facilities, this safe village will merely be a drop in the ocean. If we really hope to deal with this epidemic, we must establish hundreds more of these safe centers throughout America and the world.

As far as I can discover, only seven specialized facilities for rescued girls exist in America—just *seven* facilities whose staff are specifically trained to meet the needs of girls rescued from commercial sexual exploitation. If this is the best we can do here in America, poorer developing countries have even less chance of properly caring for rescued children.

We must open our eyes to what's happening in America first so we can establish enough appropriate facilities to rehabilitate these damaged children and see their innocence restored. Once we're able to implement useful strategies and proper care in the U.S., we can start spreading our expertise to other nations. It's crucial for us to lead the way in this field, especially when we consider one poignant fact: the majority of children trafficked in the United States are underage Americans.

The fact that we live in a world where children and young girls have to start over because vile, wicked people took their innocence and, ultimately, their lives can be suffocating. I'm incensed by the evil that pervades our earth.

19

Standing Up to Evil

*Hope itself is like a star—not to be seen in the sunshine of prosperity,
and only to be discovered in the night of adversity.*
CHARLES H. SPURGEON

On one of my early visits to Cambodia, I met two people who would become my heroes and with whom JOY International would form a strong partnership: Don and Bridget Brewster, the founders of Agape International Missions (AIM). Their ministry was geared primarily toward preventing children from being commercially sexually exploited as well as rescuing, restoring, and reintegrating those who had been abused.

I told the Brewsters about the work I was doing and how I was researching the needs and possibilities in Cambodia to see how JOY International could expand into the country. Having watched many documentaries and films about the plight of abused children in Cambodia and having previously visited there a number of times, I truly (and somewhat naively) believed that child trafficking in that country, while still a problem, was greatly diminished. I was astonished and heartbroken when Don and

Bridget informed me that child slavery was not only thriving there but had actually increased.

For various reasons, child sex slavery had simply been driven deep underground. The Brewsters told me that each month hundreds of children were trafficked into Cambodia from surrounding nations such as Vietnam and Laos. Sex tourists were on the increase as well, because the media focus on trafficking in Cambodia had served as a magnet for foreign predators. This is why documentaries such as the one Gail and I had watched were a double-edged sword. My heart had been torn, and I had been moved to action; certain others had selfish and nefarious motives.

Despite the grim outlook in Cambodia, Don and Bridget were excited to hear about our rescue methods. They were also impressed that our efforts always worked toward the arrest of all the traffickers, brothel owners, pimps, and pedophiles. Our conversation ultimately morphed into a strategy brainstorming session on how JOY International's techniques could be effective in Svay Pak and beyond.

A Critical Lack of Heart

One reason I had come on this trip to Cambodia was to visit the director of a global organization also involved in rescue work. This meeting had been scheduled for many months, and I was excited about the possibility of working with a strong and well-organized group of likeminded people. This organization did wonderful, legitimate work around the world. The combination of their clout and my "trench wisdom" could mean tremendous trouble for the trafficking world.

I hurried to the meeting, anticipating a powerful convergence of minds all willing to work together to plan the greatest number of rescues and arrests possible. I also decided to share with the organization's director the new strategies cooked up during the meeting with the Brewsters.

My excitement quickly waned. When I arrived, a representative brusquely told me that the director was unable to meet with me, as she was busy with other matters. I had been highly recommended by this director's predecessor, so this woman's lack of interest left me surprised. I had spent several thousand dollars and traveled more than ten thousand miles to be there. In a weak attempt at appeasement, the receptionist scheduled a meeting for me with another representative within the organization. Since I'd come all the way here and spent so much of my partners' money to do it, I figured I needed to try to make something productive happen with this individual.

We met at a local coffee shop, but after only a few moments, I wanted to walk out. I sensed in the assistant a critical lack of heart for these abused children. The young man gave me the impression that there was no hope for our team of devoted rescuers to be used in any way. He was turning down help from a team of men who were willing to risk their lives to save children from lives of horror and pain. I was entirely heartbroken and, quite frankly, rather offended. Had I wasted my time flying to Cambodia? After the conversation I was left wondering if I was wasting my time trying to fight this crime against children in Cambodia. How quickly my hope had dissipated since my talk with the Brewsters the day before.

Som Pas

After a nearly sleepless night, I decided the next morning to tour the Tuol Sleng Genocide Museum in Phnom Penh. I had brought two guests with me on this trip, and it made sense to take them to the museum and then the Killing Fields a short distance outside Phnom Penh so they could learn about the horrific period in Cambodian history when dictator Pol Pot had ruled.

Tuol Sleng is in a former high-school building that Pol Pot's Khmer Rouge used as a security prison between 1975 and 1979.

In this place of horror, thousands of Cambodians, including women, children, and babies, were horrifically tortured and killed as part of one of the largest and most hideous genocides in the history of mankind.

While my guests toured the museum, I excused myself, still struggling over the unmet expectations of the day before. Outside, sitting on a tree stump under a beautiful lilac tree, I silently reflected. God must have seen my sad heart. Without any prodding from me, a group of Cambodians appeared and came around me.

A young girl, about twelve years old, sat next to me and said, "I learn English for one year." I nodded my commendation. We exchanged names and began to chat. Once the young lady had established where I was from, the conversation soon turned to why I was barefoot. It seems my bare feet are what had drawn her and her family to me.

Her grandfather took a seat on another stump, right next to mine. He seemed fascinated by the cane I carried and signaled to me that he wanted to inspect it. I showed him how it folded up, and we all laughed together as I demonstrated how it snapped back together again to form a walking stick.

By this time about twenty people had gathered near me, and it appeared to me as if they were two Cambodian families who were also visiting the museum. I was as interested in them as they were about this barefoot, cane-toting, white-bearded Westerner.

The old Snuggles the Clown character in me couldn't resist—I had to entertain my impromptu audience. I happened to have one of my old magic tricks with me, so with a sudden flourish I pulled out a red silk scarf. With a dash of dramatic flair, I made it appear out of nowhere. They oohed and aahed.

I showed them my empty left hand, closed it into a fist, and slowly stuffed the scarf inside it. Turning to the grandfather who was seated beside me, I motioned for him to blow on my fist. He obliged. With another dramatic burst of motion, I slowly opened my hand to reveal—nothing!

The elderly gentleman responded with a look of complete surprise, followed by a roar of laughter. He took my hand with a puzzled look, turning it over and over again, unable to believe that the scarf was no longer there. He took my other hand and did the same thing, only to find both hands completely empty.

The look of pure joy on his face truly touched my heart. He couldn't stop smiling. Of course, when I closed my fist again and asked him to blow on it once more, his eyes twinkled with expectation and disbelief. When I opened my hand to reveal the scarf, the laughter all round was even louder and more jovial.

Cambodians traditionally greet each other with the palms of their hands together, in a manner resembling prayer. Their hands move to their chest, and they bow slightly, a form of greeting called *som pas*. Generally, the higher they raise their hands and the lower they bow, the more respect they're showing. When the group was about to leave, the grandfather stood up and, facing me, offered the traditional *som pas* greeting of departure. The inflection, however, was of the highest degree of respect as he moved his hands to his forehead and gave a deep bow. I reciprocated—and then embraced him with a tender hug.

After my new friends left, I was alone again, in the same spot where these families' ancestors had been so violently abused more than thirty years earlier. I looked around and felt a little emotional. My thoughts rushed back to the discouraging meeting the day before, and in that moment I sensed the presence of the Holy Spirit. Then God spoke to me, challenging yet tenderly comforting me as He affirmed the deep calling I had been given: *Who are you? You are not acting like the man I called to rescue these children. The man I called would never question what he is called to do, nor would he doubt if he were in the right place. He would not allow one difficult meeting to stop him from doing what he knows to be right. He would not allow My enemy to deter him. The man I called would be motivated to action in a powerful way. That is the man I called to fight this crime against the children I created. You, My son, are that man.*

A river of tears flowed from my eyes as God reminded me of the violence still happening to the children of Cambodia. This time thousands of children being abused in the vilest way imaginable—not by Pol Pot and the Khmer Rouge regime but by men from all over the world who traveled to this country for the express purpose of renting children's bodies to satisfy their sick desires. Children whose ancestors had been so violently abused right where I sat.

The abuse suffered in Cambodia under Pol Pot lasted four years, wiping out millions of lives. The oppression of the Khmer Rouge ended in 1979 with an invasion from Vietnam. People inside and outside Cambodia finally stood together to fight the dictator and his oppressive regime. I knew that until people once again rose together to fight the evil of our day, the sexual abuse of children would continue to destroy lives—not just in Cambodia but throughout our world.

20

A Heart That Weeps

If to be feelingly alive to the sufferings
of my fellow-creatures is to be a fanatic,
I am one of the most incurable fanatics
ever permitted to be at large.
WILLIAM WILBERFORCE

Over the years various people have suggested that I am obsessed with rescuing children out of the sex trade. They have gone on to label my work my "cause."

My cause? I wonder. Friends have told me there are other causes in the world, and I shouldn't get upset if people don't join me in this fight. If you're nodding your head in agreement—if this is truly what you think—I won't be offended if you put this book down right now and join the fight to save the whales instead. Of course, I also encourage you to at least finish reading this chapter to help you put into context my obsession. Before I share more stories, I want to give you a better understanding of why I do not consider my work a *cause* but a *calling* on my life and why I feel so strongly about it.

There are so many things wrong with our world and so many good causes we could choose to champion. People strive to make the world a better place for monkeys or gorillas or some species near extinction. They throw their energy and resources into saving porpoises or sea turtles. Closer to home, many people spend huge amounts of time and money rescuing abused dogs and cats (we've all been affected at some point by those heart-wrenching television commercials). Then we have our feathered friends in need of our protection—eagles, hawks, owls. I find animal abuse despicable, and I fully believe we should be better stewards of the earth God has given us. But is any cause anywhere near as important as God's call to minister His love to the broken and dying—especially when it means saving a child from being repeatedly raped ten to fifteen times a day?

Hard Truth

Every time I think of the reality sex-trafficked children endure, my obsession grows, and my heart breaks a little more. If you have been able to conjure only a vague idea of what this might entail, then please allow me to say it again: children between four and seventeen years old are often forced to "service" ten to fifteen men a day, every day. These children must engage in penetrative sex with these depraved men who are acting out their pedophiliac perversion.

Sometimes enslaved children are considered too young by their child brokers to have intercourse, so they're forced to perform oral sex. Yet some child brokers are so ruthless that they allow even toddlers to be brutally raped. Regardless of the child's age, however, intercourse is generally allowed as soon as someone is willing to pay for the so-called honor of breaking a girl's virginity. If that's not sick enough, once a girl's hymen is broken, abusers will often sew her up and sell her as a virgin multiple times. Young boys don't escape either; they're sodomized as long as the price is right.

To put the problem (and my subsequent passion) into perspective, JOY International once rescued a girl who was held captive by one of the most evil and brutal gangs in America. Being Satan worshipers, the gang ensured she repeatedly fell pregnant by rape for the sole purpose of sacrificing her babies to Satan. The human mind struggles to comprehend such darkness. The term "breeder" is used in the trafficking industry to distinguish these young women from other sex slaves.

Other babies are born into a different fate. My experience working with rescue teams has introduced me to horrific realities. When they discover a girl is pregnant, some Indian traffickers allow certain sex slaves to bear children instead of forcing an abortion. They welcome the newborn child as an additional source of income.

From infancy they educate the child, training him or her to perform sex acts on men. The child is taught to perform various sex acts without intercourse until their owner is ready to sell their virginity for an astronomical price. As a result, these children carry no guilt for the acts they're taught to perform, and traffickers see this as an added bonus because these children are easier to handle. As far as the child knows, performing sex acts is what she was born to do. She doesn't think she's doing anything wrong or unnatural.

Some girls are kept for the sole purpose of becoming pregnant. Brothel owners sometimes deem certain slaves less physically desirable, so they put them to use as breeders. Children born to these slaves will never know the meaning of a normal, loving family. All they know is human depravity and a life of slavery, their experience of life ultimately equating to a grim semblance of hell.

How men can stoop to such depths of degeneracy is beyond human comprehension. I continue to be shocked each time I hear how depravity just continues to descend deeper. This is where we see Satan in his full-blown form, completely undisguised—in-your-face evil!

This is graphic information, but I can't apologize for offending people's sensibilities. Child rape happens every single day because good people turn a blind eye instead of doing something about it. This is why it upsets me when people try to convince me that rescuing whales, gorillas, or any other animal is more important than rescuing a child or woman from sexual abuse!

God's Truth

If the hard truth isn't enough, let me offer God's truth. Abuse of human beings should be our number-one cause for one simple reason: God has made humans in His image! Every child is God's personal creation. Scripture tells us that He knows each child intimately even before the child is formed in his or her mother's womb: "Before I formed you in the womb I knew you" (Jeremiah 1:5).

God has filled His Word with verses that declare He's the Creator of *every* child *ever* born. This is why we call Him our heavenly Father. Parents are the tools God uses to bring children into the world. But only God gives life. Throughout Scripture He reminds us of this basic truth:

> Did not He who made me in the womb make them? Did not the same One fashion us in the womb? (Job 31:15)

> Behold, children are a heritage from the LORD, the fruit of the womb is a reward. (Psalm 127:3)

> You formed my inward parts; You covered me in my mother's womb. (Psalm 139:13)

> Thus says the LORD who made you and formed you from the womb. (Isaiah 44:2)

To change the world, we must first change the way we see it—we must change our worldview. If you're a Christian, this means striving to become more like Jesus and loving each person unconditionally, especially children who are unable to fend for themselves. Literally millions of God's children who have been trafficked are waiting for this change to take place within the church. They are waiting for us to answer their cries.

Luke 4:18 tells us that Jesus came to set the captives free and that He has designated you and me to be His voice, His hands, and

His feet. He paid the price for our spiritual release from captivity. It's up to us to release these children from their captivity and endless nightmare.

Am I obsessed? Maybe I am. But I don't consider my dedicated focus a cause; it's God's call on my life. Actually, I prefer to call it my passion. I'm passionate about fighting for a child's freedom. I have to be true to my life experience, and for me, as I have said so many times wherever I have spoken, awareness without action is apathy. I have looked into the eyes of so many children rescued out of bondage. I've held some of them in my arms as they shared their stories and wept on my shoulder. Knowing that millions more children in our world are experiencing the same pain fills me with a holy compulsion to do everything in my power to rescue them.

One Child at a Time

I love what has become known as the starfish story. It has several versions, but my favorite comes from the essay *The Star Thrower* by Loren Eiseley. In it he describes a renowned writer who walks along the beach each day before starting work. One morning the writer noticed a younger man along the ocean's edge engaged in a perplexing exercise. The young man was picking up starfish and throwing them into the ocean. It seemed pointless, because the beach, stretched out for miles ahead of him, was covered with tens of thousands of starfish. The writer approached the young man, asking why he was throwing starfish into the ocean.

"Well," replied the young man, "the sun is up, and the tide is going out. If I don't throw them in, they'll die."

"Do you not realize," the writer asked, "that you cannot possibly save all these starfish? There are simply too many of them. What difference can you make?"

Without pausing, the young man bent down, picked up yet another starfish, and threw it into the ocean. As it splashed into the water, he said, "It makes a difference for that one!"

The older man decided to abandon his writing for the day and spent the morning throwing starfish into the ocean.[1]

After every rescue I have a picture in my mind of a child's face. The face is blank, without any detailed features. I visualize flowing hair around the face, but that is the only feature I see. I wonder, *Which one is next? What does she look like? What is her name? Where is she, and what must I do to set her free?*

I have wonderful relationships with each of my seven grandchildren. In February 2006 my first granddaughter was born. When I held Emma in my arms for the first time, something changed inside me. She touched my heart in a way no other person had; I was holding the daughter of my daughter. While watching her play in my home one day, the thought suddenly struck me, *What if she were kidnapped and forced into this nightmare? What would I do to rescue her?* An icy shiver ran up my spine, and I knew the answer immediately: *Absolutely anything!* Lying in bed that night, I was overcome by an experience I can only describe as supernatural. I heard words similar to those I had spoken to the pastor in Cambodia, but this time God was speaking these words to me: "Jeff, if you would do anything to rescue your grandchild, would you do anything to rescue My child?"

The answer can be seen through a question someone once asked my wife: "Why do you think God called Jeff to do this work?"

She immediately responded, "God knew Jeff would say yes."

I often weep when I share the stories of these children, regardless of how much I try to control my tears. I sometimes cry uncontrollably. I always make a concerted effort to keep my emotions in check, however. In fact, at times when I'm about to share a story that makes me weep, I say to myself, *No tears this time. I'm not going to cry!* Yet often when I say this, the floodgates open even more widely.

One night in the town of Kampong Cham, Cambodia, I was an emotional wreck after meeting a six-year-old girl who had been raped multiple times in one day (she was rescued on the way to the brothel where a child broker had planned to sell her). I couldn't stop weeping. But I have always been prone to strong emotion, from the time I was a child watching Shirley Temple movies. It makes me who I am. That night I cried out to God, "Father, why am I like this? Why do I get so emotional?"

That night in Kampong Cham, God answered me in a clear and loving way: "My son, I've given you eyes to see these children the way I do, and I've given you a heart to feel for these children what I feel."

Since that moment I've never questioned my tears, because I don't cry alone. My teardrops are mingled with God's. We both weep for the least of these. The call and passion of my life are His, and we are searching for and bringing home *His* creation, one rescue at a time.

21

Abolitionist

It is not light that we need, but fire;
it is not the gentle shower, but thunder.
We need the storm, the whirlwind,
and the earthquake.

FREDERICK DOUGLASS

An abolitionist is a person who favors the abolition of a practice or institution. The term is generally used to depict people who take a stand against slavery, but the simplest definition I have found is "a person wanting something to end."[1]

In the context of this meaning, I readily accept the title: Dr. Jeff Brodsky, abolitionist! I state with the utmost conviction that I wholeheartedly want to see an end to the commercial sexual exploitation of children, teens, and young women.

In this role I do all I can not only to rescue children but also to open people's eyes to the horror that child sex slaves experience daily all over the world and urge them to follow Jesus' mandate to care for the least of these. If I can motivate one person to action, many more children can be saved.

Right Here in This City

One Sunday morning in 2011 I visited a church in Phnom Penh, the city where I first saw the barefoot children and made my barefoot decision. This church was one of the largest and most diverse in the city. I used a headset to hear the translation of the Cambodian pastor's message, spoken in the Khmer language. After the service I searched out the pastor to meet him.

"I'm Jeff Brodsky from the U.S.A.," I told him.

"You Docka Brosky?" he said to me in broken English. "Oh, is my pleasure to meet you. I always want to meet you for long time!"

I was a bit surprised. I wasn't aware he had heard of me. We exchanged a few pleasantries, and I told him I had really enjoyed his message. Then I said something that came as a shock, both to the pastor and to me. I can only surmise that the Holy Spirit was speaking through me.

"Pastor, can I ask you a personal question about your message?" I asked.

"Personal?" he said, surprised.

"Yes, a personal question," I nodded.

"Sure, no problem," he agreed, his voice betraying slight concern.

"I really enjoyed your message," I continued, "but my question is, do you really believe what you preached this morning?" The question sounded a little rude, even to my own ears. I usually never ask people something like this.

He looked at me quizzically. "Do I believe it?"

"Yes," I replied. "Do you believe what you preached about this morning? Did you share your message from the 'know' or the 'flow'?"

"I don't understand what you ask me," he said, shaking his head.

"When you teach from the 'know,' you simply put together an expository message from your head. When you preach from the 'flow,' you're preaching from the overflow of what God is doing in your life and heart. Which did you teach from? The know or the flow?" I must reiterate that I was shocked at the words coming out of my mouth.

After thinking for several seconds, the pastor looked at me and said, "This is a very good question. I never hear this before. I think I give this message from a little of both. A little know and a little flow."

"Great!" I said. "Let me ask you another question."

At this point I noticed genuine worry showing on his face. He was probably sorry he had said yes the first time. I continued, undaunted.

"In today's message you told us about Paul and Silas being in prison—they were praying and singing hymns. An earthquake caused their prison doors to open. You were reading from Acts 16, is that correct?"

At midnight Paul and Silas were praying and singing hymns to God, and the prisoners were listening to them. Suddenly, there was a great earthquake, so that the foundations of the prison were shaken; and immediately all the doors were opened and everyone's chains were loosed. (Acts 16:25–26)

"Yes," he said, nodding in agreement.

"Pastor," I said, "the same God who released Paul and Silas from prison is looking for an opportunity to release many more prisoners who are being held captive right down the road from this church."

His eyes widened with surprise.

"Right here in this city," I continued, "young girls are being used as sex slaves. They are in a different kind of prison from Paul's and Silas's. Some of these children are as young as four years old. They are the most abused children in your country. The abuse they suffer is even worse than what your people suffered in the 1970s when the Khmer Rouge tortured and killed Cambodian citizens. Their torture may have lasted hours, days, or even weeks, but these children are tortured multiple times a day, every day of their lives. Some are tortured their entire lives, even into adulthood."

The pastor was mesmerized. My words were getting to him.

"These innocent children do not have the faith of Paul and Silas. They do not know how to pray and sing hymns with the kind of faith that will release their shackles and open their prison doors. They are unable to simply walk out and be set free. These children have lost all faith and all hope. They have nothing more to believe in. They're just trying to survive the nightmare that is their life. My brother, God has given you the power to set these children free. You are highly respected in this city, and Pastor, you can rally more than a hundred churches that can march to the places where these children are held captive. Together you have the power to set them free and tell them about Jesus unlike anyone else in this city."

He looked at me in wide-eyed amazement as he listened to the words God had given me to share with him.

"How can I do this?" he asked. "How can I set them free?"

"You mentioned during your message this morning that you have two daughters." He nodded. "If one of them was kidnapped and you found out she had been sold into a brothel and forced to be a sex slave, what would you do to set her free?"

"I would do anything," he replied earnestly.

"Well, God wants to know, if you would do anything to rescue your own child, would you do anything to rescue one of His?" I said gently.

His face scrunched up, and he began to weep. I embraced him as he cried for some time. The Lord was touching his heart. He regained his composure and looked directly into my eyes.

"You have challenged me more than any man in my life," he said. "I don't know what I can do, but I will try to do something."

I don't know if this pastor ever followed through and did anything to rescue trafficked children in his city, but I like to think he made a decision that day to accept the challenge. In truth, though, I can only hope that the seeds I planted took root in him and that he and countless others are now bearing fruit. That's sometimes all I can do.

In Good Company

When I think of being an abolitionist, it's humbling to have my name associated with others who have truly fulfilled this role in a powerful way. The work of these individuals led to the freedom for many thousands who had been slaves and unashamedly called others to action as well.

Harriet Beecher Stowe, for instance, the author of *Uncle Tom's Cabin*, was reportedly called by President Lincoln "the little lady who started the big, bloody war." Her novel forever changed how Americans viewed slavery, galvanized the abolitionist movement, and influenced the culture at the outbreak of the Civil War.

Harriet Tubman, a former slave who bravely ran from her owner in the south and made her way to freedom in the northern U.S., is alleged to have said, "Freedom for myself is not enough." She became a conductor on the Underground Railroad[2] and eventually an armed scout and spy for the Union Army; her actions brought about the rescue of her family members and many hundreds of other slaves.[3]

Frederick Douglass, another former slave turned abolitionist, spoke openly and passionately against slavery, both in America and in England, often putting his life at risk. Several years ago I had the privilege of meeting Dr. Kenneth Morris, the great-great-great-grandson of Frederick Douglass and the great-great-grandson of Booker T. Washington (founder of Tuskegee Normal School for Colored Teachers, now Tuskegee University). Continuing in the tradition established by his ancestors, Dr. Morris is carrying the torch of emancipation lit many years ago by speaking out against human trafficking.

After a dramatic encounter with God, William Wilberforce fought vehemently and tirelessly to abolish England's slave trade.

And Abraham Lincoln, America's sixteenth president, passed the Emancipation Proclamation to end slavery in America. Today Lincoln routinely polls as the best president in history.

Others have fought valiantly, and many have lost their lives wanting to end the injustice of slavery. Did they win? No, but the war rages on. These heroes did achieve the enactment of laws making slavery a crime. Their fight at least made it illegal to own another human being.

Even More Widespread Today

While we celebrate what Lincoln did, the stark truth is that slavery didn't end in 1865 with the Emancipation Proclamation. Not only does slavery still exist, but today it is more widespread around the world than it was during the early centuries of slavery in America. As one of the largest and fastest-growing crimes in our world today, slavery is thriving.

These days slavery is called by another name: *human trafficking*. Although it has a new branding, I assure you it is still slavery. People are bought and sold, oppressed and brutalized.

Some think I'm exaggerating when I say slavery is growing exponentially unlike at any other time in history, but consider the statistics. It took three hundred years to export twelve million slaves from Africa to the Americas.[4] Right now, in 2018, one hundred and fifty-four years after the Thirteenth Amendment to the U.S. Constitution passed and seventy years after article four of the United Nation's Universal Declaration of Human Rights banned slavery and the slave trade worldwide, slavery is now worse than in every other period in history *put together*.

Estimates vary, but at the writing of this book, one report states,

> The latest global estimate, according to the International Labour Organization (the United Nations agency that

deals with global labor issues), calculates that nearly 21 million people are victims of human trafficking worldwide. Roughly 4.5 million of those victims are trafficked for the purpose of sexual exploitation.

The International Labor Organization also estimates that 55 percent of all trafficking victims and 98 percent of sex trafficking victims are women and girls.[5]

The International Labour Organization also states that 150 billion dollars a year is generated through forced labor, with two thirds of that (U.S. 99 billion dollars) coming from commercial sexual exploitation.[6]

This illicit industry has overtaken arms trafficking to become the second-largest black-market industry behind drug running.[7] That's not the worst news. It is also the fastest-growing global industry.[8] Human trafficking is on track to overtake the sale of illegal drugs and become the number-one largest illegal industry. Unfortunately, human trafficking is *big* business.

How is this possible? How can any nation turn a blind eye to this crime against innocent children?

When I preach against these atrocities, people sometimes suggest that I tone down the language I use. They prefer to hear, "The commercial sexual exploitation of children is widespread," rather than, "Almost ten million children are being raped for money." But I prefer to state cold facts rather than obscure the terms with comfortable sociological jargon. No matter how we choose to define or label the crime, these children are forced sex slaves. They are enslaved for the sexual gratification of customers who pay their captors to rape them in relative obscurity.

If you think I'm being dramatic, think about the horrors of slavery in America alone—the indelible scar it has left on two continents. Now think about that crime being perpetrated against children in the form of sexual abuse.

Can We Win This War?

I would be overjoyed to see the scourge of child exploitation completely eradicated from the face of our planet. I have committed my life to fighting it, to continuously searching for the least of these who are trapped in an endless nightmare. Currently, however, there aren't enough police in the world to rescue twenty-seven million trafficked individuals, nor do we have enough post-rescue facilities. My goal is to bring us closer to a future free of human trafficking, one child at a time. In some raids only one child is rescued; other times ten are rescued; other times, I have seen as many as eighty-nine set free from sex slavery.

We must fight for every last one, especially when it's the outright sale of a child. Alone I can and certainly will rescue some children. As people join me in this fight, however, we could double, triple, or more greatly multiply the number of children we can rescue by working together. I don't care who gets the credit, as long as a girl gets rescued and God gets the glory.

22

The Right Word

Without dignity, identity is erased. In its absence,
men are defined not by themselves, but by their captors
and the circumstances in which they are forced to live.

LAURA HILLENBRAND

One day I had the opportunity to express my convictions in front of an incredibly influential—and intimidating—group of people. My friends John-Michael and Ellen Keyes invited me to speak at a national school safety symposium they were hosting geared toward first responders. John-Michael and Ellen are founders of an organization called the I Luv U Guys Foundation,[1] named for the last text message they received from their daughter, Emily. In 2006 Emily was tragically murdered by a lone gunman who overtook the Platte Canyon High School in Bailey, Colorado, just a few miles from where I live.

Upon entering the huge room, I saw that it was filled with several hundred official-looking people. Many were law enforcement personnel who had flown in from all parts of the country, including some officers from the New York Police Department and even Scotland Yard in the United Kingdom. Also there were teachers and educators, lawyers, prosecutors, and attorneys general.

When John-Michael and Ellen had invited me, I had thought, *Does the work I do really fit into this mix of professions?* But trusting that God and the Keyes knew what they were doing, I had agreed to come. Still, I was as nervous as could be, since I was to follow Sergeant A. J. DeAndrea, who worked with the Arvada, Colorado, sheriff's department and had been a first responder during the Columbine High School massacre in 1999 as well as at the Platte Canyon High tragedy. Sergeant DeAndrea exuded manliness; he bulged with muscles and had not a smidgeon of body fat on him. At his side he wore a holstered gun, flanked by a Taser, mace, and a pair of handcuffs. This guy was the real deal. As he showed a video of actual responders during these infamous emergencies and tragedies, all I could think was, *Holy mackerel, I have to follow this guy? Lord help me!*

I was so tense that I almost texted my wife to call me and make up an emergency. At that point I heard him say, "Men, one of the keys is being in tiptop shape!" And here I was, this fat old grandpa who looked like Santa Claus. *Now I have to get up and speak after that?* My insides churned.

When John-Michael went onstage to introduce me, he told this audience full of official people, "I'm going to do something I've never done publicly." Then he sat down on the edge of the stage, removed his shoes and socks, and said, "The man I'm going to introduce to you has been barefoot for three years [this was in 2013]. I'm sure he'll tell you about it, but in solidarity with Dr. Brodsky, I'm removing my shoes and socks while he speaks."

I climbed the stairs to the stage and looked out at the sea of faces, staring at my audience as they waited for me to start talking. Then I looked directly at Sergeant DeAndrea sitting in the front row, larger than life and full of vitality, and said, "That was phenomenal, Sergeant! I wish you had followed me instead of me following you." A few people smiled. "When Sergeant DeAndrea was up here," I said to the whole crowd, "he said that we men have to be in tiptop shape. Obviously that doesn't apply to me." More smiles and a few chuckles.

"Physically, we're two completely different types of men, but emotionally, Sergeant DeAndrea and I have something in common when it comes to our jobs and our calling in life: we both care about the victim. Our first priority is the victim and making sure the victim is safe. Agreed?"

Sergeant DeAndrea nodded.

D, not *S*

"I need to show you guys something," I said. "Look at this headline in yesterday's local newspaper."

The headline flashed across the auditorium screen: "150 Prostitutes Busted!"

People immediately started applauding and calling out their congratulations.

I allowed a weighty pause. "If you feel good about that, shame on you!" The applause immediately died.

"Why do you feel good about busting the victim?" I asked. "Those women are victims. They are not prostitutes—they are *prostituted*. Replace the *s* at the end of the word with a *d*. They are prostituted for the profit of others."

The room was deathly silent.

"Why are just the women busted? Why aren't their pimps busted? Why aren't the johns who pay to violate them busted? Why aren't these girls offered a chance at another life? These one hundred and fifty girls who have been prostituted, why are they not *rescued* rather than busted? We shouldn't feel good about that headline!"

I pointed to my shoulder. "This shoulder has captured the tears of more girls who were prostituted than the police have ever arrested. I listen to their stories; I don't look at what they do. I can see some of you shaking your head and thinking, *You don't know what you're talking about, because when we arrest them, they curse us, spit at us, flash their breasts at us, offer their services to us, call us every name in the book.*" Some of the law enforcement officers nodded.

"They're trained to do that; they're manipulated." I pointed to my head. "Their minds are owned by their traffickers, and they are brainwashed into believing their traffickers can see them. You have to ignore that and not look at *what* they're doing but *why* they're doing it. Then you need to embrace them in a way that shows you care about them. That precious teenage girl or young woman has to believe that you're going to make sure she's safe. That you're not going to put her in a prison cell, but that you're going to make sure a social worker is available to her."

I had their attention.

"I can assure you, not one of these women when she was a little girl thought, *I can hardly wait to grow up so I can sell my body to multiple men every day. I can hardly wait for them to slap me, beat me, spit on me, urinate on me, ejaculate on me, and make me feel like garbage. I'm really looking forward to being raped several times every day by filthy, stinking, drunken men and beaten or even drugged and tortured if I don't obey.* Not one of these women ever had these thoughts!"

My words were having an effect.

"Let me prove to you that this was a rescue, not a bust," I continued. "Any of you have daughters? If one of those one hundred and fifty women were your daughter who had run away and had been approached by a pimp who then forced and manipulated her into becoming a prostitute for him, would this have been a bust, an arrest, or a rescue?"

A soft murmur rippled through the audience.

"You already know the answer," I told them. "People say to me all the time, 'Why are you so obsessed with fighting child trafficking and exploitation? It's not your child.'"

I surveyed my audience, knowing my next sentence might not resonate with all of them.

"I don't want to put my beliefs on you, but I believe that every one of those one hundred and fifty women is God's child, His creation. Not one of them should be treated like second-class citizens, especially by law enforcement. We need to embrace these women and young girls and show them they're victims. For whatever reason a woman is doing this, it's rare that she actually desires to be a prostitute. Something happened in her life whereby she was forced, coerced, manipulated, or put into a position where she felt she had no other choice and had to comply to survive.

"The majority of these women and young girls, well over 90 percent and closer to 99.5 percent, I would estimate, are women who have been prostituted for the profit of someone else. Until we make one important change in our country, we'll always have this problem: *we must embrace these girls as victims and not as criminals.* We must put the real criminals in prison! Forget high-priced lawyers and plea bargaining; if a guy traffics a girl for commercial sexual exploitation, he should go to jail for X number of years with *no possibility* of parole.

"You start doing that, and just watch how the statistics change. We can put an end to sex trafficking when we start arresting the right people. When we start treating the people who are committing these criminal acts as criminals and start rescuing the victims they prey on. That's why I'm barefoot. Until every child in the world is free from the risk of bondage and the endless nightmare of sex trafficking, I will remain barefoot."

Not in a million years would I have expected this crowd to flock around me after I stepped off the stage. I could barely get down the stairs. When I finally did, a gigantic police officer intercepted me. I call this man "Hercules"; like Sergeant DeAndrea, he didn't have an ounce of body fat anywhere on him, and all his muscle was covered in tattoos. From his height of six feet four inches, he looked down at me and boomed, "Dr. Jeff! I'm really ticked off at you!"

Trying to ignore the huge pit in my stomach, I gazed up at Hercules and said, "I'm really sorry. I just shared what I believe to be the truth."

"Nobody makes me cry!" he burst out. "I'm sitting there bawling my eyes out, and I'm looking around, wiping my eyes, making sure none of my buddies see me."

I blinked in surprise.

"Then I notice they're all crying too," he went on. "I can promise you this, after what you said, as long as I'm wearing this uniform I'll never, ever look at those girls the same way again."

I smiled and heaved a sigh of relief, but the last thing he said really stuck in my mind: "Every cop in America needs to hear what you just taught us."

Two Million Right Now

As I said that day during the symposium, no woman ever dreamed of being prostituted when she was a little girl. Through more than twelve years of work in this industry, I have met many young women rescued from a life of terror, and not one of them has said it was her choice to go into the sex trade and service ten to fifteen men a day for almost no money, enduring being beaten, starved, drugged, and often violently raped.

In a tiny number of adult prostitution cases, the rare woman (or man) becomes a prostitute by his or her own volition. Even so, this choice often stems from hanging out with friends with loose morals, running away from home, and becoming addicted to drugs or alcohol or both. To feed their addiction, those in this situation can wind up prostituting their bodies. I've found that almost all adults who willingly prostitute themselves have made a series of bad life choices, often forced by terrible circumstances and manipulation.

That is not the case with children who are sexually exploited. *Every* child I have ever found in the child sex trade was either kidnapped or sold and forced into a life he or she never chose. In fact, the term "child prostitution" is a paradox; using these two words together is flat-out absurd. How can anyone call a child of four, eight, or twelve a prostitute? These children are nothing but slaves used for two reasons: to satisfy the unnatural desires of men who are, arguably, the sickest people on Earth and to provide financial gain to people who have no conscience or compassion whatsoever.

My heart breaks knowing that as I write these words, somewhere in our world children are being used in unspeakable ways. Right now more than two million children are experiencing heinous crimes against them. It's time to get drastic and make a scene—to pull out all the stops—even if we don't see immediate results.

23

The Barefoot Mile

It's not always that you get to see your money or your effort,
the seeds you plant, actually bearing fruit.
ANNIE LEAVITT

As I walk in solidarity with trafficked children by going bare-foot, I continually encounter people who are moved by my story. Through them God has blessed me in ways I never could have imagined. But that's how God works. When we obey Him, He increases our joy in unconventional ways.

A pastor in Ecuador insisted on washing my feet and, while doing so, gently caressed and kissed them. It was a truly humbling experience. Throughout my years of traveling barefoot, I have had my feet washed many times.

On another occasion a rabbi in New Jersey not only allowed me to attend a synagogue service barefoot but also introduced me, a Messianic Jew, to his staff. During the service he also had me come up to the bimah (the podium in the center of a synagogue from which the Scriptures are read), knowing that everyone would see my bare feet. When I left the platform, he embraced me and whispered in my ear, "It was an honor to have you at my bimah this morning. You are welcome here any time."

Then there was the college student who went barefoot for a week; his life was dramatically changed. The same was true of a high-school student who went barefoot for thirty days in December in Colorado and the high-school students who went to their prom barefoot.

The First Barefoot Mile

Perhaps the most notable experience I had regarding my bare feet was at a church in Coshocton, Ohio, where the JOY International Barefoot Mile was initiated.

I had been barefoot for three years when I shared my story with about two hundred people at a small-town church in Ohio in 2013. When people hear my story, they're always fascinated that I've been barefoot for so long. This time was no different. But what happened after I shared my story with this group was a first.

A few days after I spoke, I received a call from Kelly Treat, the church youth pastor, telling me that the church's youth group had called a meeting to discuss how they could help raise funds for JOY International. One of the teens had had a stroke of genius and suggested that the youth group "walk a mile barefoot in solidarity with Dr. Jeff."

"I love the idea," I said, immediately recognizing the immense potential in it.

"Is there any way you can come back here and be a part of it?" Kelly asked.

A bit tongue in cheek, I replied, "You raise five thousand dollars in pledges, and I'll be there!"

Well, they did, and I flew to Ohio to walk with this incredible team. About a hundred barefoot walkers took part that day in Ohio, and together they collected more than ten thousand dollars! I broke down as I spoke to these people that day, as I found it incredibly humbling that they would walk in solidarity with me. I had never thought of my going barefoot being used as a fundraiser. I had gone barefoot purely for personal reasons.

Seeing the success of this walk, the idea struck me: *Would other people be interested in walking a mile barefoot to raise funds?* JOY International started testing the concept on social media, explaining why and how we proposed to host Barefoot Mile walks, to see if people were interested. We had such a tremendous response that I contacted Kelly Treat, who had first called me from Ohio with the idea, and asked her if she would consider being a national director for the Barefoot Mile. She was already well qualified. She said yes and was our national director for the Barefoot Mile for more than a year. She also went to Cambodia with one of our teams.

JOY International has since hosted many Barefoot Mile walks all across the U.S., traveling as far as Alaska to host them. In July 2015 we even hosted one in Cambodia for my five-year "barefoot anniversary." On the day of that event, the skies opened up, and rain poured down. We figured the turnout would be significantly reduced, but by the time we finished the walk, we had almost eighty walkers. "Can we walk with you?" people asked as they saw our group walking barefoot and discovered why we were doing it. "This is beautiful!"

From what I could tell, most of the participants that day were Cambodian nationals. These men and women whose ancestors had endured so much at the hands of the Khmer Rouge took off their shoes and socks to walk barefoot for their country's children. When I saw that, I decided to return to Cambodia every year to celebrate my barefoot anniversary by walking a Barefoot Mile with the Cambodian people.

The Barefoot Mile has become a global event, raising hundreds of thousands of dollars to help JOY International with rescue efforts. I regularly challenge people to "walk a mile barefoot." That challenge seems easy to some, so I also encourage people to go barefoot for a day. In fact, I encourage you right now to just try going barefoot for twenty-four hours. Get up from your bed one morning, and don't wear any shoes or socks until you wake up the next day. You'll be amazed at the interesting and challenging day you'll have, especially if you venture out into public areas!

When I decided to go barefoot, I didn't see it as a fundraising tool. Fundraising simply developed when others saw being barefoot as an opportunity to help us with expenses for rescue operations.

A New Identity

I was walking the Barefoot Mile with a group in Lansing, Michigan, when Mary caught up to me and asked if she could tell me something personal.

"I'm a former prostitute," she began.

"No, you aren't. You were not a prostitute!"

"Excuse me?" she replied in astonishment.

"You were never a prostitute."

With a hint of disbelief, she stared at me and said, "How can you say that? You don't even know me."

"Sure I do. I may never have met you personally before today, but I know all about you, and I can assure you that you were not a prostitute."

Sounding a little wounded, Mary asked, "Why do you keep saying that?"

"Can I ask you a question?" I said, shifting to a gentler tone.

"Okay," Mary nodded.

"Did you have a pimp?"

"Yes."

"Did you give him all the money you received from your clients?"
She nodded.

I looked into her eyes as we walked side by side, and with great compassion I assured her, "Like I said, Mary, you were not a prostitute."

She still didn't catch my drift.

"You were not a prostitute, Mary. You need to add a *d* to the end of the word, because you were *prostituted* for the profit of someone else. Your pimp used you for his benefit—for his greed. He either forced, coerced, or manipulated you into prostitution, which means you were not a prostitute, Mary. You were *prostituted*."

The realization flickered in her eyes.

I continued, "I'm sure there was the odd occasion when you were caught and arrested by the police, right?"

"Yes," she nodded.

"Well, no matter how the police looked at you or how they treated you, Mary, you were not a criminal. You were a victim. Do you understand?"

Tears welled up in her eyes as she whispered, "Oh my gosh—I've never heard anything like this before. It completely changes everything about the way I see myself."

We stopped walking for a moment as I watched the revelation change this young woman right before my eyes.

"Thank you so much for sharing this with me, Jeff. I'll never forget what you've just told me."

As we came to the end of the Barefoot Mile, Mary gave me a hug, her face radiant with a big smile. It had been a precious time with a beautiful sister in the Lord, who now had a greater understanding of the abuse she had endured as a victim of trafficking.

That day, standing there with me, Mary received the complete revelation of her new identity. She understood that she did not have to carry the heavy burden of a false identity any longer. She was free and brand new—washed in the blood of Jesus Christ. Each of us can do the same thing for anyone who has ever been trafficked for sexual slavery.

How to Make a Waitress Weep

I was a little nervous as I prepared for my recent flight to Anchorage, Alaska. It was February 2018, and needless to say, temperatures in Alaska in February were rather low. But I had many meetings scheduled to prepare for the fourth annual Alaska Barefoot Mile that would be happening on May 19, so I braced myself for winter in the Last Frontier and planned to be extremely careful with my feet while I was there.

I never let weather or location determine where I will go, as long as my going to a place will help further our efforts in the rescue of children, teens, and young women who are trafficked. No compromise! Despite my apprehension about the weather in Alaska, I looked forward to my meetings there, as we planned to make the upcoming Barefoot Mile even more successful than previous ones, in one of which Donna Walker (the wife of Alaska governor Bill Walker), Anchorage mayor Ethan Berkowitz, and U.S. senators Lisa Murkowski and Dan Sullivan joined us.

My first full day in Alaska, it was minus two degrees. I walked into a restaurant for breakfast, and my waitress, Linha, looked at me (actually at my feet) in surprise. But she didn't say anything. When she gave me the bill, I put my "Why Am I Barefoot?" card inside the payment folder with my credit card. A few minutes later Linha came back, very emotional, and shared with me about how her family had come from Cambodia and escaped the Khmer Rouge. Wow! Linha couldn't stop thanking me for the work I do. Then she asked if she could hug me. I had been dreading being in Alaska in the winter, and here God was, bringing the right person at the right time to show me how blessed I was in the calling He had given me. Praise God from whom all blessings flow.

Later that day I went out for a late lunch. My waitress, Atsuko, was astonished when she saw me barefoot. I gave her one of my "Why Am I Barefoot?" cards as well, and about fifteen minutes later she came back to my table in tears and insisted on buying my lunch. I tried telling her that it wasn't necessary, but she said she wanted to bless me like I bless the children. You guessed it—my tears began to flow. I couldn't rob her of a blessing, so I allowed her to buy my lunch. She too hugged me. I was truly, truly humbled.

"Yes, Lord, I hear You loudly and clearly," I prayed. "Thank You for the privilege, honor, and blessing of serving You these nearly forty years."

I have met many wonderful people the world over, both those who are on the front lines of the fight to end human trafficking as well as the children and women we have rescued or tried to help. But added to these two groups are the many men, women, and children I've met who have become aware of the gravity of child sex slavery through seeing an old grandpa with bare feet and have responded with their whole hearts to help in some way, whether little or big. I'd had nothing planned for that day—I was simply having a day of reflection and rest as I prepared for a week filled with a myriad of meetings to prepare for yet another Barefoot Mile. Yet God used two touching moments to remind me of the life He had called me to. I love the way God uses the simple things for powerful reminders of His call and touch on our lives.

24

What's Your Why?

The two most important days of your life are the day you were born
and the day you find out why.
MARK TWAIN

When I first began rescuing sex-trafficked children, I did anything within reason to earn money, both to support Gail and me and also to contribute to the ministry we ran. I have rarely received a salary from a secular job in the thirty-five years since I founded JOY International. I have simply done whatever I could to keep my family afloat and the ministry operational.

For a while, however, I was involved with a network marketing company, and I slowly, methodically climbed the earnings ladder. It didn't take a genius to realize that success at work would increase the balance in my bank account, which in turn would enable me to rescue more girls. My only motivation in making as much money as possible was to support my ministry.

The Stockdale Paradox

One year the company held a conference, and because I was having a pretty good financial run, they invited me to speak. They asked me to talk about the "why" behind success. Specifically, they wanted me to stir all the employees to ask themselves, "What's my why?" They wanted each person to ponder why he or she wanted to be successful.

I accepted the challenge, but I knew that my personal reason for wanting financial success was most likely vastly different from everyone else's reasons. My approach to this would take some finesse.

The marketing company I worked for had been promoting a program encouraging employees to reach a specific level of achievement within ninety days. Of course, this goal was virtually unattainable. The aggressive timeline and target were, respectfully, a crude tool the company was using to try to motivate employees to become super achievers as fast as humanly possible. No matter how hard people worked at achieving this ridiculously high watershed, not even 5 percent of the employees made it in the ninety days allotted. I did reach the goal, although not in ninety days; it took me one hundred twenty days. But then I hadn't really tried to reach it in the prescribed timeframe—I wasn't after the company's prize. I reached the goal only because I was driven by a different motivation than the other employees were: to increase the number of rescued children.

As I researched the topic for my presentation, I discovered the story of U.S. Navy Vice Admiral James Stockdale, one of the highest-ranking U.S. officers captured during the Vietnam War. He was kept as a prisoner of war in the infamous camp known as the Hanoi Hilton. Reading Stockdale's story, I saw a correlation between the message I had in mind and the mind-set the vice admiral had maintained when he was in captivity. His mind-set has actually been captured in the term "the Stockdale Paradox."

I chose a daring direction for my speech: I would contrast my personal motivation for success with the company's stipulated goal of attainment and, using the Stockdale Paradox, emphasize the difference between the two models.

The day of the conference, I was next to last to present to the room of about five hundred serious businesspeople. All the speakers before me were really good, and as I sat listening to them, nervous thoughts plagued me: *Oh my gosh, I have to follow these guys? They're all professional businesspeople, and here I am, a minister who happens to be in this business to make some extra money. I'm not a businessman!* (These were the same feelings I'd had during the safety symposium full of public officials and law enforcement—I seem to have a knack for finding myself in fish-out-of-water situations.)

I reminded myself that I would be talking about God and wouldn't hide anything. I would simply tell the people what I believed. Then, of course, the guy before me delivered an outstanding speech to a roar of applause, and my anxiety soared again. My stomach was in knots, to say the least. I had always been comfortable speaking to thousands of people in a church, but in front of a group of intimidating businesspeople, I felt totally out of my element. I gathered myself, walked up onstage, and, after congratulating the other speakers on their remarkable messages, began.

"I don't know if this is what you're looking for," I said, looking out at the expectant faces before me, "but I'll just share what's on my heart, and hopefully you'll get something out of it."

I took a deep breath. "I don't know what your why is. I have no idea why you hope to achieve this specific level in the ninety days expected of us."

With a sweep of my hand I included the entire audience in the question I now asked: "How many of you have tried to reach this level in ninety days? Raise your hands." Everyone raised their hands.

"How many of you actually made it?"

Out of the five hundred, two people raised their hands.

"Were the rest of you disappointed on day ninety when you realized you weren't even close?" Demure nods of agreement rippled through the audience.

"How many of you know people who didn't achieve their goal in the ninety days and quit their jobs as a result of this perceived failure?" Between fifty and sixty people raised their hands, which likely meant the company had lost that many people due to their unmet expectations.

"Let me share a story with you," I went on, "about a man named James Stockdale and tell you about how I believe his story applies here."

I explained to my audience that Stockdale had been the highest-ranking officer captured as a POW during the Vietnam War. I told them how a vast number of men also captured within a similar timeframe committed suicide only months after their capture. Many others lost their minds and were subsequently killed by their captors. But James Stockdale was different. He was a survivor. Prisoners were separated to prevent communication, so in an effort to sustain morale and retain sanity, Stockdale initiated an ingenious method through which he and his fellow prisoners were able to communicate. His system used Morse code, but the delivery methods were subtle: banging on the building's internal piping system, tapping on walls and doors, even humming and whistling. Of course, this system had the extra benefit of keeping the prisoners' minds occupied. But that was not the most important factor distinguishing Stockdale from the others. Stockdale had a specific image engraved on his mind—a singular mental picture that set him apart from all those who lost their sanity or committed suicide.

"When they entered the camp," I told my audience, "most prisoners tried to anticipate a particular date on which they hoped their captivity would end. *I'll be out by Christmas*, the new arrival would promise himself. *My release from this hell will be my Christmas present.* Christmas would arrive and pass, and he would still be a prisoner of war. *Well, okay,* he would think, *in just a few more weeks I'll be out of here. On New Year's Day I will be released.* New Year's Day would come and go, and the soldier would still be there, imprisoned in an enemy camp. *I'll be out of here by Valentine's Day*, he would think, or, *I'll be set free by my birthday*. Every time the specified day arrived without the prisoner having attained his desire, it brought him down a notch, increasing his state of depression with every disappointment.

"Jim Stockdale never set a date. He simply knew that one day, no matter how long it took, he would attain his goal."

At this I paused, allowing my eyes to slowly sweep across the corporate crowd before me. I was pleased to see every face riveted on mine, compelled to discover Jim Stockdale's secret.

"Do you know what his goal was?" I asked. "His goal was to see his wife and children again."

Many in the audience registered surprise. "That's it! It didn't matter when. He wasn't focused on how long it might take. He was just determined to see his family again."

I saw some realization dawning throughout the crowd.

"Stockdale refused to allow the foreign power holding him captive to intimidate him into losing sleep or cause him stress over the timing of his release. He would not allow the prison guards to bully him into losing his mind. These were decisions Stockdale actively chose. It didn't matter what tactics his captors used as long as he remained focused on seeing his wife and children again. He chose to center his reality on the knowledge that eventually he would achieve this one basic but profoundly meaningful goal he had set for himself. One way or another, he would ultimately be reunited with his family."

Certain to Reach the Goal

"What's your goal?" I asked my audience. "What is keeping you sane? How are you moving forward? Why do you want to attain this elevation to upper management?"

I let them mull over their individual answers to these questions for a few seconds. Then I pointed to certain individuals, asking each of them, in turn, to raise a hand so that the group could identify them before they answered.

"Tell me," I prompted, "what are your goals? There are no wrong answers. Nobody here will judge the goal you aspire to. What is it that you ultimately want?"

Several people responded predictably. One guy had a strong desire to become a millionaire. He planned to take the first step by earning one hundred thousand dollars that year. He spoke about how he planned to increase his earnings annually until he finally reached a million in assets and cash. Another man had his heart set on a yacht. Another wanted to own a sailboat. These different aspirations revealed the essence of each heart's desire, and the desires were valid. Nobody judged them. Having firmly established the platform I needed, I prepared to reveal my own why.

"This is great," I began. "Each of you has a specific dream you're following, and looking at this talented crowd, chances are good that all of you will achieve them." I paused. "The thing is, my goal is very different than all of yours. Because of this significant difference, I cannot fail to reach my goal. In a way, my goal is much like James Stockdale's in that his goal was never really about him. He knew how much his wife and children needed him; he was certain they longed to see him as much as he did them. His goal centered more on his family than it did on himself. Similarly, my goal is not about me. My heart is centered on reaching another group of people."

I had the group's complete attention now, and I started my slide presentation. Images of young children flickered across the screen.

"Children just like these all around the world are being used in the most vile and degrading manner imaginable. At this very moment, somewhere in the world a child is being used for commercial sexual exploitation. In fact, all around the world, children are suffering this atrocity right now. I'm talking about children from seven to ten years old, sometimes even younger! Children are being used as sex slaves, raped multiple times every day to satisfy the sick desires of depraved men.

"You want to know my goal? My why?" I looked out over the crowd.

"I live, breathe, and work to set these children free!"

Not a paper rustled.

"Everything I do in this company is based on the number of children I can free from slavery. This is my motivation for reaching a certain number of clients, as it enables me to attain a stipulated level of income. This in turn means I will earn that much more money, which translates into setting more children free. That's why I'm standing here today. This is my why."

I walked off the stage.

The place erupted. For about seven minutes my audience gave me a deafening standing ovation. I wept uncontrollably. The last thing I had expected was for these people to respond in such a way. (I had actually half expected to be booed.)

The conference manager, George Veronis, was set to speak next to close the event, but when he finally stood up and approached the microphone, he looked bewildered.

"How do I follow something like that?" he asked. "If you're not motivated to action after what Jeff Brodsky just said, there's nothing more I can add to motivate you. I'm scheduled to speak for the next forty-five minutes, but quite frankly, this conference is over. I'm done. We're all done here today. Go home. I'm not even going to attempt to follow that."

Yes, it was an exhilarating feeling to know that I had shared my deepest truth, and the fact that it had been overwhelmingly embraced added to my emotion.

So let me ask you the question I'm sure you've been pondering throughout this chapter (and book): what is your why? Could the rescue of child sex slaves be part of your why? Is there another "least of these" for you?

Read Matthew 25:34–40 again. The least of these—the lowest of the low, the hurting, the oppressed, the violated, the enslaved—who are they for you?

The truly profound thing is that your why is connected to God's answer. It's time to take action!

25

The General and Me

It is not great men who change the world,
but weak men in the hands of a great God.
BROTHER YUN

Tomorrow I fly to Cambodia. Again.

Gail will drive me to the Denver airport, and I will board United flight 143, nonstop to Tokyo. After twelve hours and ten minutes in the air, I will have a layover of eighteen hours and ten minutes. I will get a hotel room, try to catch some sleep—but rest rarely happens these days. The last leg, another six hours and fifty minutes on an airplane, will put me in Phnom Penh at three thirty on a Friday afternoon.

Flying halfway around the world takes a toll on me physically, but it has become routine. So has answering questions about my bare feet along the way. Some of the United crew will no doubt recognize me, which helps and encourages me. I have become a regular on the Denver to Phnom Penh route.

I look forward to every trip, hoping I will be able to rescue more children from sex trafficking. By now you have a sense of my heartbeat for these children. I would go anywhere, anytime, if it meant another young girl might be free.

But this trip, like my last few, is different from previous ones. A new door for ministry has opened for JOY International, and it will likely mean trouble for traffickers.

On this stay I will spend time with one of the highest-ranking generals in Cambodia. He and I have bonded in the most unusual and unexpected way. Not only that, but he has partnered with my team to fight sex slavery in a way we could only have dreamed about a few years ago. What we have joined together to do will mean liberty for literally thousands of children—in Cambodia and around the world. This is not a pipe dream. It is already happening.

I am nearly leaping with excitement—and that is quite a sight. Let me explain.

SWAT Teams

In 2012, I stopped participating in hands-on rescue operations myself and turned my focus to police training. For one thing, my bare feet drew attention to me and increased the danger of people recognizing me. But besides that, I reasoned, who better to be the tactical team on the ground than locals who not only know the culture but also the politics and lay of the land?

Quickly it became clear that I would need help in this new endeavor. What I have in passion, conviction, commitment, and frontline experience, I equally lack in tactical skill. Simply put, I am not a trained SEAL or special-ops agent.

This is where Robert came in. He became JOY International's director of global police training and tactical operations.

Robert was a pastor for twenty-four years. He was also a chaplain to prisoners, some of whom had been prostitutes or involved in organized crime. When they left prison, he helped these people find safe houses. As Robert worked with individuals who had been involved in the world of sex slavery, God began prodding him with the why question and pointing him toward the problem of child sex trafficking.

As a pastor, he did what he could to help victims of trafficking, focusing on prevention, awareness, and local needs. But the deeper he dug into this matter, the more he realized how few were taking action to help free immediate victims. Robert felt moved to hands-on rescue work; he knew God was calling him to action to help the victims of child sex slavery. So he stepped down from his role as a pastor in obedience to God's new call on his life.

Awareness without action is apathy.

So Robert surveyed the possibilities for action. He determined that he could either join a local police force and hope to be assigned to its anti-trafficking unit, or he could train as a private security specialist. He opted for the latter. The preparation was grueling: training by a former Navy SEAL, special-operations courses, personal security detail certifications, and anti-terrorism training. In fact, during the Counter Response Group's four-week hands-on counter-terrorism instructor course, a number of students dropped out after the first day. Not Robert.

"I would rather die than quit," Robert said. "If I quit, then child sex-trafficking victims could die. If I can't handle training, how could I help in a real situation, which would be much more difficult?"

I cannot tell you how overjoyed I was to have a man with Robert's heart, skill, and drive join my team in 2017.

When I first met Robert, he was already training Cambodian police. The door had opened for him through our mutual friend Eric Meldrum, who works with the Brewsters at AIM as their director of investigations and of the AIM SWAT team. Meldrum, in turn, had built a strong relationship with Cambodia's interior ministry penal police chief, Lieutenant General Mok Chito. The general ranks high in the national government and oversees enforcement of all anti-trafficking laws. Meeting with him, according to Robert, is like meeting with the vice president of the United States.

Before joining JOY International, Robert instructed Cambodian police in basic skills, such as subject control and arresting techniques, using a tactical baton, applying first aid, and defending themselves when attacked. He trained about two hundred officers.

When he joined JOY International, the type of training he did shifted and expanded. He began specifically training the local Anti-Human Trafficking Juvenile Protection Police (AHTJPP) and SWAT teams, in cooperation with AIM, in advance tactics for the rescue of those trapped in sex slavery. These men now carry out local rescue operations.

The SWAT teams work in concert with the AHTJPP, but they actually work for AIM. This partnership enables them to conduct legal raids. It also helps these men personally. Most police officers in Cambodia have two or three jobs. It is not like here in the States; in Cambodia they work for the police force only when they are called upon. The average salary of a police officer there is two dollars a day. They cannot survive on this salary. So working for AIM helps everyone.

What JOY International does is fund the training Robert gives these men as well as the equipment for each task-force member. Each man who graduates gets to keep his gear.

AIM has two operational SWAT teams as of the writing of this book, but more will soon be in place. Since 2014, these two teams have rescued nine hundred victims. Nine hundred! I cannot tell you how that moves me to tears (although you probably already guessed that). If two teams can rescue nine hundred victims, imagine how many ten or twelve teams could rescue!

Not only that, but if this can be done in Cambodia, imagine what can be done in other nations! JOY International's tactical operations team is prepared to go into all the world to give specialized training to anti-trafficking police.

Cambodia was what is called a tier-three country—an international rating reflecting their human rights record. Tier three is on the low end of the scale. They have since moved up to tier two with a desire to reach tier one, and General Mok Chito is passionate about making this happen.

Graduation Ceremony

Every training Robert conducts lasts about two weeks, and each one winds up with a graduation ceremony. In the summer of 2017 he carried out a training under the umbrella of JOY International and AIM SWAT, and I flew over to join him.

The day before the swat-team graduation, the team being trained conducted a raid. They asked me to come along. Four girls were rescued; the perpetrator was arrested.

During the raid one of the team members asked me to go into the brothel. I did, and that was a mistake. There were used condoms everywhere, and I was barefoot. But that is the kind of risk I sometimes have to take. Seeing some of these men we had trained doing this rescue was overwhelming—and worth it!

At the ceremony the next day, twenty officers and nine generals were present. The highest ranking general was Lieutenant General Pol Pithei, who is also the director of the AHTJPP.

I was asked to speak, and I did.

"Many of you can see me walking around barefoot," I began.

Cambodians are a respectful people, so no one laughed out loud, but throughout the training I had noticed soft snickering anytime I went by. These guys had probably been thinking, *Who is this barefoot weirdo?*

I told them two stories. I told of going to the dump in Phnom Penh and being so brokenhearted over the children who were barefoot that I had chosen to walk barefoot in solidarity with them—and still did so today. And I told them how every time I bring a group to Cambodia, I take the team to the Killing Fields, where much of Pol Pot's genocide took place and where I am reminded of the great suffering and grief the Cambodian people were subject to under the cruel dictator. The expressions on the faces of these macho policemen softened.

I continued, "Atrocities against the Cambodian people still go on today—against their children and against the children of neighboring nations such as Vietnam and Laos. These children are undergoing terrible torment as sex slaves. That is why I am standing here before you. That's why we spend thousands of dollars to train you. This, my friends, is why I am barefoot."

I returned to my seat.

General Pol Pithei followed me at the podium. He appeared close to tears.

My interpreter, sitting beside me, began whispering to me as the general spoke. "He is saying that what you said really touched him. He is sharing about his mother and father."

The general looked straight at me and continued to speak. "He says he has never had more respect for any man than that man right there," my interpreter whispered to me. "He says, 'My mother, my father, during the Pol Pot regime, the Khmer Rouge, when they killed millions of our people and so many fled into the jungles, my father and mother ran into the jungle. They had no time to take anything. And they lived in the jungle, barefoot.'"

He looked around at the men. "They had no choice," my interpreter conveyed to me, translating the general's words. "This man has a choice, and he goes barefoot for our people."

As he walked back to his chair, General Pol Pithei embraced me. That moment created an incredible bond between the two of us.

All the officers after that treated me with great respect. I'd had no idea of the details of people's lives during the Khmer Rouge. What I heard that day fundamentally changed the way I saw my being barefoot.

Renewed Passion

While I was on that same trip, the general told me a story that shocked me. I had thought I had seen and heard it all, but this new evil disturbed me greatly.

In Cambodia, Thailand, Laos, Burma, Vietnam, China, and across Southeast Asia, criminals are harvesting children. They purposely impregnate young girls as well as older women who are not desirable. They let their children grow to a certain age; then, some they kill in order to harvest and sell their vital organs, while others, particularly girls, they train to satisfy men sexually. As the children who are allowed to live grow, sexual deviance is all they know. They have no conception that what they are doing is wrong. Since the general shared this with me, I have discovered that this is happening in India and many other parts of the world as well.

When I learned of this, my thoughts went in one direction: *What can JOY International do to fight this?*

We are starting strategic planning now. Things are so much worse than what most people realize. We have no conception of the depths of depravity that motivate people to brutalize their fellow human beings, especially children, in our world today. It rips my heart out.

This is why you will never see Jeff Brodsky put a sock or shoe on his foot ever again.

This is why I have been barefoot for seven and half years and will remain so for the rest of my life. This is what brought me from where I was as a little Jewish kid in Brooklyn to being a Messianic Jew who travels the world fighting terrible evils. This is what took me from watching *Heidi* to running JOY International and rescuing children whose freedom has been taken from them.

I challenge you. I don't challenge you to be me, but I challenge you to be *you* in doing something to make this world a better place for people who are suffering, whether it be a child who is trafficked or a person who has AIDS or a woman who is being abused or a baby who has been born so her body parts can be sold.

Who is your least of these? If you don't have one, please accept mine. But it's more important that you find yours. Read Jesus' words again, and match your heart and actions to the list that makes up the least of these. Then go, make this world a better place.

When will your search start? What will you do to help win the fight against evil? What will move you from where you are today to where God wants you to go?

While you think about that, I have a flight to catch.

Appendix A

Do Something!

The world is a dangerous place, not because of those who do evil,
but because of those who look on and do nothing.
ALBERT EINSTEIN

"Jeff, how do you keep from being jaded, especially after seeing victim after victim, case after case, day after day?"

I am sometimes asked this question, especially if people know that on a daily basis I receive dozens of news articles related to every area of child sex trafficking, including child prostitution, child sexual abuse, and child sex slavery. I receive a copy of all information shared *anywhere in the world* about these areas of trafficking, whether by newspaper, TV news broadcast, blog, or website.

Admittedly, it can be overwhelming. But I believe the reason I don't become cynical is because I'm focused on the task at hand. I have fresh hope each day that another child will be rescued. Maybe one child, maybe several. Maybe even hundreds. If not today, then hopefully tomorrow.

If I allow myself to become jaded, the one child who may be rescued through our efforts may remain a sex slave for the rest of her tortured life. If this one child spends just one more day in a brothel, it's one day too long. I must use the tools at my disposal to set another child free, no matter what it takes.

A former colleague of mine, the late Dave Duell, liked to say, "It's too late to wait!" This expression has never been more apt than when it involves the commercial sexual exploitation of a child. If I didn't see a light at the end of the tunnel, I would be in constant darkness and severe depression. I have to keep my eyes focused on whatever needs to be done to reach that light.

Doing Something

"Why does God allow this horror to take place?" I get this question a lot.

My reply: "He doesn't! We do. *We* are responsible for either the spread or abolition of sexual slavery."

After that people usually say, "Surely God has an answer to this rampant evil."

My response is the same: "*We* are God's answer!"

You see, each of us has to make a decision to actually do something. This doesn't necessarily mean that you have to be barefoot for the rest of your life or go undercover into brothels, KTVs, and dance bars, risking your life to rescue children. In fact, I'm not suggesting you join a rescue team and go undercover. Most of the team members we work with are either current, former, or retired law enforcement or special forces military personnel. Rescuing children is extremely dangerous and takes more than just courage—it takes specialized skills.

But we must all simply do what we can. Are you a good businesswoman or businessman? Are you an organizer who can put together a fundraising event and make people aware of the war we're fighting? Every skill and weapon is valuable if it helps rescue one more sex slave.

My primary goal is to motivate people to *action*—whether it's a group of ten, one hundred, or a thousand people. If I don't manage to motivate at least one person to action, then I've failed. As long as it motivates people to action, I'm prepared to spend the rest of my life walking barefoot, just as I'm prepared to spend the rest of my life searching for another child who suffers this horrific abuse.

Of course, as I mentioned earlier, action comes in various forms. It could mean:

- A commitment to financial support, whether it's a one-time gift or a monthly gift to JOY International or one of our partner organizations
- Putting together a Barefoot Mile or coming up with your own idea to raise funds (even kids can participate in this!)
- Writing your legislators to request mandatory sentencing of sex offenders
- Going on a short-term missions trip with JOY International
- Inviting me or others to speak with your church, civic or social group, business colleagues, or school or college
- Committing to pray for those going into dark places to rescue those in slavery
- Spreading the word about what JOY International and other real rescue organizations are doing to rescue children from bondage

Regardless of how you become involved, I urge you to do *something*! In John's Gospel we read the red letters of Jesus: "Whoever has this world's goods, and sees his brother in need, and shuts up his heart from him, how does the love of God abide in him?" (1 John 3:17).

We are the body of Yeshua, our Messiah. We are His hands, arms, legs, and feet, and we are also endowed with His mind. It's up to us to set the captives free and put our enemy to flight. We are the righteousness of God in Yeshua, and He has commissioned us to fight for justice for the least of these.

If you have contributed to the freedom of the least of these in any way, then I say, "Rejoice!" Have you donated money to a rescuing organization? *Rejoice!* Have you prayed for the organization's successful rescue operations? *Rejoice!* That's what I call teamwork. TEAM is my acronym for "together everyone achieves more." Working together means that the victims win, the bad guys lose, we store up riches in heaven, and God receives the glory! We truly succeed by the grace of God.

Whether or not you decide to actively start rescuing children, you can be involved. All I ask is that you do *something*.

Because your silence is your consent.

Awareness Can Exacerbate the Problem

I get a little weary of hearing some organizations and celebrities talk about child trafficking. Hundreds of groups and just as many celebrities are jumping on the child-trafficking bandwagon as if it were some new cause. Most often these people have no idea about what an actual rescue involves. They just babble on about how terrible the situation is because it's the cause *du jour*. I'm sure many believe that their efforts are making a difference because they're making people aware of the problem, and celebrities even host major fundraisers that bring in millions of dollars and make more people aware.

What these organizations that focus primarily (or only) on awareness fail to understand, however, is that *they're actually hindering rescue efforts*. That sounds counterintuitive, but anyone on the frontlines doing rescue operations will tell you it's true. Here's why. When public awareness increases without corresponding rescue mobilization, brothel owners simply take the children deeper underground, making it more difficult for real rescue organizations to find them. In fact, these types of awareness efforts actually increase the demand for child sex slaves by making predators aware of the areas where children are available.

A prominent TV personality produced an exposé resulting in both scenarios: predator awareness was increased, and brothel owners took their child sex slaves deeper underground. Even though this celebrity does good work overall, I wrote to his company to tell him he had escalated the problem and why. But my words were ignored. So at the time I didn't say anything further.

No more silence! When I see injustice or a hindrance to true rescue work, I'm not just going to speak about it. I will shout it out to make people aware of the truth. Sometimes truth hurts, but not nearly as much as the pain a child feels every time he or she is ravaged.

I sometimes wonder why God doesn't simply say to Jesus, "Son, go and fetch Your bride; take her out of there. The time has come. I've had enough." Yet we labor under the illusion that if we only make people aware of the problem, we have somehow become part of the solution. We might just as well simply click a "like" button on Facebook or Twitter for all the good we're doing.

To all those organizations that only care to make people aware of the problem, I plead with you to go beyond awareness! In this book I shared my longtime mantra: *awareness without action is apathy*. Take real action to help free another child from a brothel. These children do not need to be talked about; they need to be rescued. Every moment we just talk is another moment of pain, horror, and abuse for trafficked children.

To individuals, I beg you to give your time and money to an organization that isn't just talking about child trafficking but whose members are actually risking their lives to go undercover and bear an exorbitant financial burden to rescue children from their endless nightmare.

One highly sought-after female speaker engages emotionally with women around the world, raising funds by talking about the horrors of child trafficking and the need to rescue children from brothels. But when I interviewed her director of operations and recorded our discussion on film, he emphatically stated that they are *not* involved in rescues. He told me they don't even have homes for rescued girls because it would be too much work and too costly to hire workers. I have to wonder, *Well, what on Earth are they raising money for?*

On the other hand, I know of sincere, effective organizations that actually send undercover teams into brothels to rescue children from their living hell. As I mentioned in chapter 14, one of our own undercover Indian field operatives was severely beaten and hospitalized when a brothel owner discovered his true identity. Two weeks later he was back undercover with me, working the brothels and dance bars in search of underage enslaved girls. This kind of gritty determination makes a difference. At JOY International we can't just *talk* about child trafficking and child sex slaves—we have to do whatever it takes to actually rescue these children.

How Much Is She Worth?

No matter how many women and children are rescued, the setup costs for a rescue are usually pretty similar, regardless of how many girls we rescue; the cost of post-rescue services, on the other hand, corresponds to the number of rescued girls.

For example, we once received a report that a criminal syndicate was holding two underage girls in Mumbai. So we arranged to raid their place of business. The operation cost about two thousand dollars to arrange. But while the police were leading the two girls out of the brothel, one started screaming hysterically, "More girls! More girls! There are more girls in there! If you move the dresser, you'll see a secret door—they're hiding more girls in there!"

Immediately the police went back in with the team. They moved the dresser, saw the door it was covering, broke it down, and found *thirteen* more girls! After that particular raid, the cost of essential post-rescue services obviously increased with the increase in the number of girls rescued. I've never been so happy to see the costs add up!

While setup costs are usually pretty similar for each country, there are exceptions to the rule. I told you in chapter 14 about a rescue operation that cost six thousand dollars to rescue one girl (Anaya). Considering that sole rescue against the backdrop of the rescue of thirteen girls that cost two thousand, was it worth spending six thousand on Anaya? It was to her. If it were your child who was forced into the child sex trade, working in a brothel and servicing ten to fifteen men a day, would it be worth six thousand or even six hundred thousand? You would sell everything you owned. When it's not your child, it's much easier to look the other way.

Yet if we could see every child as God's child, we would soon love every one as we do our own children. I told you this earlier, but I must reiterate my why: years ago God asked me, *If you would do anything for your own child, would you do the same for one of Mine?* How could I possibly say no?

A Curable Disease

The problem of child trafficking isn't like lung cancer or leukemia that causes doctors and scientists to search for a future cure. This is a disease we have the ability to cure today. JOY International has proven this fact time and again. Our methods just have to be applied on a much greater scale, which is ultimately dependent on greater financial input.

Rescue operations are costly. Our teams have travel and operating expenses; they need surveillance equipment. And that's just the beginning. After they're rescued, the children need rehabilitation and reintegration. This is one of the primary reasons so many organizations only *try* to carry out rescues. When they realize the actual expenses and dangers involved, sadly, they stop doing and go back to talking.

An interviewer once asked me, "Jeff, if you had unlimited funds, what would you do?" My answer was immediate: "I would establish rescue operations in countries across Asia, Southeast

Asia, Africa, Central and South America, and Europe. In the United States I would fund anti-trafficking task forces and work with organizations to establish safe houses for the thousands of girls who would be rescued. Unlimited funds would mean unlimited rescues around the world, setting millions of captive children free while putting the perpetrators in prison."

I am astonished by the inordinate number of letters, e-mails, text messages, and calls I receive from all over the world—South Africa, Uganda, Kenya, Morocco, Mozambique, and many other countries in Africa and the Middle East. People across the Caribbean, Central and South America, Europe, Asia, and Southeast Asia are all asking for help to fight child trafficking. They all beg me to help them set up rescue operations for trafficked children in their countries. The sad truth is that without funds, I cannot possibly help all these people.

I'm a visionary. Imagine if all the churches around the globe joined forces to tackle this problem in their local areas. If we simply started doing what God commands us to do in His Word, we could set these captives free. If we started giving to our local churches what we're asked to give, our churches would become empowered to rescue more children.

I'm often struck by a common global irony: we tip servers at restaurants a higher percentage (usually 20 percent) than the tithes we give to our churches. Under Mosaic law, Israel was expected to tithe 10 percent of their harvest or income to the Lord so that the Levites and others serving in the temple could do God's work efficiently. Many modern Christians, operating on the same principle, also give 10 percent of their income to the church, yet they have no problem giving a food server a tip equaling 20 percent of their restaurant bill. Please don't get me wrong. I encourage you to give servers 20 percent for serving you. I'm simply pointing out the weird logic that values a restaurant experience above the mandate of God, through whom we live and move and have our being.

We're not under the Mosaic law anymore. Through Jesus' sacrifice and great love, we have been set free from the law. We are no longer required to abide by the letter of the law; rather we are to live by the Spirit of the law. In other words, we're free to give the greatest percentage we can afford so that God's will can be done on Earth just as it is in heaven. JOY International has teams constantly on the lookout, going out every night, seven days a week, across America and around the world, searching for enslaved children, teens, and young women used for commercial sexual exploitation. They're always ready, at a moment's notice, to go anywhere in the world in search of children needing rescue. All they need is your financial backing.

Use Your Voice

A precious young woman who was part of a youth group I led many years ago posted on Facebook about the awful reality of child sex slavery:

> I heard the most horrid thing on the local news tonight—a story about children being sold for sex! I feel sick to my stomach. I wish I hadn't heard it. It keeps replaying in my mind . . . my heart is heavy. :(

Sadly, the comments I read on her post from well-meaning friends implied that it would be better to steer clear of bad news. Their statements reminded me of the classic three monkeys who cover their eyes, ears, and mouths, respectively, portraying the sentiment "see no evil, hear no evil, speak no evil."

I felt compelled to respond to her post:

> My dear Melissa,
>
> You will always hold a special place in my heart. I read your latest post on Facebook, and based on what others

have shared with you, I have to respond to what you wrote. The advice most of your friends gave you (which I'm sure was well intentioned) regarding this subject is wrong. Very wrong.

I want to begin by sharing this verse with you from John 14:27. These are the words of Jesus: "Peace I leave with you, My peace I give to you; not as the world gives do I give to you. Let not your heart be troubled, neither let it be afraid."

Melissa, you are a gifted, anointed, precious young woman of God. When I see and read of your life with your husband and your beautiful children, my heart explodes with delight for all of you.

Yes, Melissa, there is horrible evil in the world. In the verse your friend shared (Philippians 4:8), Paul says, "Whatever things are just . . ." Turning a blind eye to the injustices in the world and ignoring them is the worst thing we can do, as it accomplishes nothing positive. As Christians, it's our responsibility to fight injustice. *Anyone* living on our planet, if they have any sense of moral decency, whether they be Christian, Jew, Muslim, Hindu, Buddhist, agnostic, or atheist, should be fighting injustice, especially when that injustice is against an innocent child.

Melissa, I believe the reason you responded the way you did comes out of the sensitive spirit God has blessed you with. I hope that spirit always stays with you. It's one of the things that makes the beautiful light in your life shine so brightly.

You are well aware of the work that I do with JOY International. I receive more than a dozen news reports from all over the world *every day* about the worst horrors and tragedies imaginable that happen to children. Sometimes it's so overwhelming that I wish God would simply call someone else to do this work. The sexual abuse and commercial exploitation of a child is the worst form of evil in our world today. Each day I hear the cries and feel the pain of children suffering around our world as they're forced to do the most despicable, deplorable, degrading, and heinous things we can possibly imagine. It literally tears me apart. As I hear the cries of these children, I remember Psalm 126:5: "Those who sow with tears will reap with songs of joy" (NIV). It's to this end that I work diligently.

Melissa, when I see one of the girls we rescue go through the healing process and then enter into a relationship with the Lord, and then I see her singing, dancing, and worshiping before God, it gives me indescribable joy. This would never happen if I took the advice of your friends— if I looked away and did nothing. Melissa, you don't have to do what I do. Some (like me) are called to go; some are called to send. But we are all called to fight injustice. We're all called to pray.

When you see (and feel) the injustice and horrors of our world, my hope would be that you would pray for the victims and perpetrators and sing songs of praise because of how blessed you are with a wonderful husband and three precious, beautiful children who are safe from harm. I know that if it were one of your daughters who were being abused, you certainly wouldn't "look the other way." On the contrary, you would give up your life to set your child free from bondage. Every one of these children is somebody's child, and every child is a child of God.

Melissa, always, always remember, it's not the sadness of our situation or the horrors of the world that we look at, but we need to "be thankful in *all* things" because "the JOY of the Lord is our strength."

Be blessed, Melissa. You're already a blessing.

Now people are different, and certain topics may affect one person differently from how they affect the next person. But we shouldn't use this as an excuse to shy away from difficult topics.

Have you ever thought that you may be more sensitive to certain issues because you could do more good work in that area than someone who's not equally affected by that particular injustice?

Instead of fearing the matter or remaining silent, we need to use our voices—one of the strongest tools we have. Our voices enable us to share truth that will hopefully educate and motivate others toward action, which can lead to the potential rescue of another child. If each of us were to reach one other person, we could change our world *in one day*. That's why we must be courageous and stand strong in our faith. We must follow the convictions of our hearts. We must *all* fight injustice, especially when it is perpetrated against innocent children. We must see it, hear it, and speak against it if we want to change our world for the better—even if the change helps only one more child.

If a person finds a specific injustice particularly distasteful, it could be the Holy Spirit prompting him or her to take action against it. Some people are horrified at the number of unborn babies aborted every day. As horrific as this and other injustices are, refusing to pay attention to the statistics because they nauseate us is not an adequate response. We need to see what is happening, and then we need to *act* on the horror we feel by speaking out against wrongdoing.

I'm not saying we should seek to fill our days with every travesty we can find. That's not what God has called us to do. But the worst thing we can do is turn off the information. Instead, we need to use our lives to make the world a better place, especially in the areas that trouble us most.

For me this comes down to human slavery, particularly sex slavery, and even more particularly child sex slavery. The idea of haves and have-nots angers me like few things can, especially when the difference between them is life and an endless nightmare of daily death.

Tell Others

When people ask, "Jeff, what can I do?" I respond the same way every time: "Do something! Do anything!" Besides giving financially, one way to help is to spread the word about JOY International.

Starting the conversation with others couldn't be easier. Just say, "I know about this guy who has walked barefoot since 2010. He does it to raise awareness for children around the world who are barefoot, hungry, and in dire poverty. And because these children are often preyed upon by traffickers and sold into slavery, he runs a rescue organization for them."

Who wouldn't be captured by that opening sentence? Encourage people to go to our website (www.joy.org) and take a look. Once they see the work we're doing, most people are inspired to become involved.

As I wrote in the preface of this book, God tells us throughout His Word that we are to champion the cause of the oppressed. A child sex slave is most certainly bent under the weight of oppression. If you ever attempt to excuse yourself from fighting for the oppressed, remember again what Jesus said about helping the least of these:

> The King will say to those on His right hand, "Come, you blessed of My Father, inherit the kingdom prepared for you from the foundation of the world: for I was hungry and you gave Me food; I was thirsty and you gave Me drink; I was a stranger and you took Me in; I was naked and you clothed Me; I was sick and you visited Me; I was in prison and you came to Me."
>
> Then the righteous will answer Him, saying, "Lord, when did we see You hungry and feed You, or thirsty and give You drink? When did we see You a stranger and take You in, or naked and clothe You? Or when did we see You sick, or in prison, and come to You?" And the King will answer and say to them, "Assuredly, I say to you, inasmuch

as you did it to one of *the least of these* My brethren, you did it to Me." (Matthew 25:34–40)

Cause *du Jour*

While writing the original draft of this part of the book, the National Weekend of Prayer to End Slavery and Trafficking was about to start. Several times I was asked how JOY International planned to leverage this prominent weekend.

Huh? I thought. *It's a* weekend *of prayer?*

What about a National Awareness Week? Or a Child Trafficking Awareness Month? Maybe we should plan a National Human Trafficking Awareness Hour or Minute—or Second? That last one would be my vote!

Forgive my irritation; I know people mean well, but seriously, is a weekend of prayer all we can manage? Conversely, it appears that child trafficking is becoming the cause *du jour*—cause of the day. This is not a bad thing in itself. It should be our number-one fight, and trafficking of children for commercial sexual exploitation should be first on our list *every day* until it's eradicated. I'm all for that! However, I'm sure God expects more consistency from us in our fight for the least of these.

Right now, while you read this paragraph, millions of children are being forced into abominable sexual acts with heartless, reprehensible people. We can (and should) do more than set aside a particular week or month to pray to God for an end to this evil. We should be praying to this effect *every single day*!

Each day I pray for an opportunity to rescue at least one more child. Not everyone can physically go out to initiate these rescues, but everyone can help *send* someone who's called to go out. Don't wait for a prayer weekend or an awareness day, week, or month. Send those who are going to the front lines! Pray for us. Pray for sexually exploited children right now, today and every day, until the last child is set free.

Never Quit

People sometimes ask me if enduring all the disappointments involved in our work is worth one successful rescue. Quite frankly, while my heart is greatly motivated by even a single rescue, the disappointments and failed rescues actually galvanize me to even greater action and inspire me with a fiercer determination to succeed in rescuing the next victim. In the world of rescue operations, every failure lays a foundation for the next successful one. I can't allow the disappointments to affect what God has called me to do.

We fight a wily, evil enemy who does whatever he can to prevent our success. Disappointment is a clear indication of the battle waged against us. Satan and his demons are focusing their energies on us. They're doing everything they can to stop us from hunting down their evil henchmen. I have no option but to approach this critical work with a warrior mentality.

A Global Move of God

What would the process of eradicating sex trafficking from the face of the earth look like? It would have to be a massive global move of God in the hearts of both Christians and non-Christians. Is that possible?

You tell me, because it starts with *you*.

After reading this book, if you're still somehow uninspired and choose to do nothing to make a difference, are you complicit in trafficking these children? Think about that. Let it sink in. The fact remains: *awareness without action is apathy*. We grow closer to Jesus by applying the knowledge He gives us. Merely recognizing evil is not enough. God expects Christian warriors to take active steps to destroy it. I'm reminded of a few pertinent verses in James 2:14–16:

> What does it profit, my brethren, if someone says he has faith but does not have works? Can faith save him? If a brother or sister is naked and destitute of daily food, and

one of you says to them, "Depart in peace, be warmed and filled," but you do not give them the things which are needed for the body, what does it profit?

Maybe Proverbs 3:27 is a little more direct: "Do not withhold good from those to whom it is due, when it is in the power of your hand to do so."

Honestly, it comes down to how much you value the kingdom of God. We can eradicate child trafficking if we just do what needs to be done (and what God has commanded His church to do).

Alone I can do a little. But working together we can win this war.

Will you fight with me? Will you do something to bring home the least of these?

Appendix B

A Little Child Shall Lead Them

Even a child is known by his deeds,
whether what he does is pure and right.
PROVERBS 20:11

A few years ago I spoke about child slavery to a junior-high group at a popular summer camp in Colorado called Camp IDRAHAJE (the name is similar to an acronym but uses the first two letters of each word in the phrase "I'd Rather Have Jesus"). (When I speak to children about the work I do, I never mention child sex slaves. I share with them about child *slavery* today and how enslaved children are forced to do terrible things.)

You may be asking, "How could tweeners possibly help in the fight against child trafficking?" Well, one twelve-year-old girl, Gracelyn, who heard me speak certainly believed she could; she didn't hesitate. At the weeklong camp she learned how to make paracord survival bracelets. When Gracelyn went home, she told her parents about JOY International and Dr. Jeff Brodsky, "this guy who goes barefoot everywhere." She told her parents she wanted to do something to help JOY International.

"I want to make a hundred of these bracelets and sell them for ten dollars apiece," she told her parents, "so I can give JOY International a thousand dollars." Some parents would try to dissuade their child from such a lofty goal, but Gracelyn's thought it was a great idea and encouraged their daughter wholeheartedly. Before long her father called and proudly told me how overjoyed his daughter was to be able to give me a check.

"Can we bring it to you?" he asked.

"Why don't you come to my home?" I replied. "Let's have a barbecue, and she can give it to me then."

Gracelyn's family came out, and we barbecued some burgers in celebration. When we were done eating, this remarkable young girl came up to me and handed me a huge check for one thousand dollars! I was blessed beyond words. She also gave me one of the bracelets she had made (I wear it every day). As I write this, I'm looking at her bracelet, smiling. It reminds me not only of what I'm doing, but also that a child roughly the same age as the girls we rescue was so deeply touched by the ministry of JOY International. She just did what she could to raise funds, and suddenly, boom! JOY International had a thousand more dollars to rescue children. Just imagine if a thousand more children in America did that.

Izac and Mr. Wiggles

During my first winter of being barefoot in Colorado, my then twelve-year-old grandson, Izac, whom we affectionately call Zee, was standing outside with me one snow-covered morning. He noticed I was experiencing some pain from the cold.

"Papa, why don't you just put on a pair of socks?" he asked matter of factly.

"Zee," I replied, "I can't do that. It would be compromise. The children I'm doing this for can't cover up their pain, so neither will I cover up mine. When I experience a little pain, it actually reminds me why I've decided to go barefoot. The pain I have will go away in a few minutes, but the pain those children have—the children we try to rescue—their pain will stay with them until someone rescues them and sets them free. Being barefoot reminds me those children are still out there."

That year Izac taught me a valuable lesson about sacrificial giving. I was in the process of leaving for a rescue trip to Cambodia. Izac had been involved in the national youth development program called 4-H, a club that teaches youngsters to develop citizenship, leadership, responsibility, and life skills. It also gives them an opportunity to raise funds toward college scholarships. Students are encouraged to raise cows, chickens, pigs, and other farmyard animals and show them at county fair auctions. The money they receive for their livestock covers the expense of raising the animals, with the balance going toward the scholarships.

Izac spent several months meticulously raising a pig, which he affectionately named Mr. Wiggles. I had grown up on the city streets of Brooklyn, New York, so this idea was really foreign to me. Not too many of my Jewish friends ever raised a pig on the streets of New York City, or anywhere else, for that matter!

I loved watching Zee raise Mr. Wiggles. It was a fascinating process, and I saw firsthand how this wonderful opportunity taught him responsibility. I watched him climb into the pen to feed, water, and clean Mr. Wiggles and, of course, have plenty of fun playing with him.

The day of the annual Park County Fair finally arrived, and Zee proudly showed Mr. Wiggles, hoping to win his first belt buckle (a big deal in 4-H and county fairs across America). Well, I thought Mr. Wiggles was just an ordinary pig, but Zee must have done something really right, because when he displayed his pig at the county fair, to my astonishment Mr. Wiggles was awarded the proud title of Grand Reserve Champion— second place overall out of all the hundreds of pigs at the fair! Not only that, having earned this impressive accolade, Mr. Wiggles was auctioned for more than a thousand dollars. My grandson took so much pride in this accomplishment. I loved seeing his excitement. The money was also a great boost toward Zee's future.

I was driving when Zee called, asking me when I would be home. He told me he had something to give me—a surprise! When I walked through the door, he didn't waste any time. He immediately greeted me with a hug and handed me a hundred dollars.

"It's for JOY International! You can use it to rescue the children," he said.

Now Zee had no idea what the children were being rescued from; he just knew his Papa was traveling all over the world to reach children who desperately needed help. I thanked him as best as I could and quickly excused myself to head into my bedroom and cry. I was overwhelmed by my grandson's generosity. Zee's heart's desire was (and still is) to help rescue children. Why they had to be rescued didn't matter. He just wanted to play his part. Not only had this young man raised a champion pig and auctioned it for a healthy sum of money, but he had also known that the most important part was giving back to those who needed it most—the least of these.

On my return from my next trip to Cambodia, I couldn't wait to see Izac and share with him how carefully I had invested the funds he had donated. I had given half of Zee's contribution (with additional funds from JOY International) to Lida, a young Cambodian woman who runs a ministry called Precious Women to rescue young women. Lida goes into brothels in search of young women, helping to free them from being prostituted. She has been highly successful in the rescue, restoration, and reintegration of young women forced into the sex trade and has also done much work toward prevention.

I gave the other half of Izac's contribution to Dr. Yem, my Cambodian friend and co-worker who fed children living off scraps from the garbage dumps. Apart from feeding them every day,

Dr. Yem also ran a special bus program. He arranged for these underprivileged children to board a beautiful bus, provided by Joyce Meyer Ministries, where they learned a basic school syllabus, sang songs, and escaped their brutal world of poverty for a few hours each day.[1] His program was also a wonderful example of the prevention model that complements rescue, restoration, and reintegration. By caring for these children, Dr. Yem helped ensure that they were not taken by or sold to criminals who would have forced them into sexual slavery.

"Zee," I told my grandson, "you've planted good seed in fertile ground. God loves to multiply seed so well sown. It was a special moment for me when you blessed my ministry with your gift, and it was even more special when I handed half of it to Ms. Lida and the other half to Dr. Yem. I don't know how God will multiply this blessing to you, but He has already blessed me beyond measure by giving me the opportunity to call you my grandson."

Since that time Zee has traveled twice with me to Cambodia to minister to children at risk.

What Can You Do?

If a twelve-year-old girl can raise one thousand dollars and my then twelve-year-old grandson could donate one hundred, what can you and your children do to help these trafficked children escape their bondage and put them on the road to freedom?

Appendix C

Host a Barefoot Mile

Christ has no body now but yours. No hands, no feet on earth but yours.
Yours are the eyes through which he looks compassion on this world.
Yours are the feet with which he walks to do good.
Yours are the hands through which he blesses all the world.
TERESA OF AVILA

The beauty of the Barefoot Mile is its simplicity. You can host or sponsor an event in your city, town, school, church, youth group, neighborhood, etc.—*wherever* you are, in *any* country!

If you would like to host a Barefoot Mile, simply go to the JOY International website (www.joy.org), and click on the "Barefoot" tab. Or you can contact our office at info@joy.org. We'll guide you through the process and show you how to set up a personal fundraising webpage hosted by JOY, which features your photo, a description of what you're doing and why you're doing it, a short video clip of me sharing the barefoot journey, and a thermometer to help you gauge your progress toward your goal and explain how people can make donations. We make the process extremely easy—no one has to collect a single dollar. You simply tell people to visit your personal webpage to donate funds.

Groups and organizations (local businesses, Kiwanis and Rotary clubs, churches, youth groups, colleges) can also sponsor walks. We've had schools, sororities and fraternities, even a football team involved in Barefoot Mile walks. At the event we did in Anchorage, Alaska, in summer 2016, the governor's wife, the mayor of Anchorage, and two U.S. senators joined us. We encourage people from all *walks* of life to participate!

Whatever you do, wherever you do it, we encourage you to tell potential supporters of your Barefoot Mile that every step they take raises funds that JOY International uses to rescue more girls. The more funds we receive, more girls are rescued. It's as simple as that.

Participating in the Barefoot Mile will bring a sense of purpose and significance to you and any group.

Barefoot Event Ideas

The Barefoot Mile concept can be adapted to fit other fun events.

We have a Barefoot Golf event in Colorado. The hosts call it Barefoot Birdies and Barbecue. People can golf barefoot (if they choose) and then after the golf event, they'll walk the Barefoot Mile, followed by a barbecue.

As an individual, you can recruit friends, asking them to sponsor or join you in the walk. You set up your webpage and recruit ten to twenty friends, then each of them receives his or her own page and finds his or her own sponsors to add to the fundraising efforts.

You could also organize the walk as a team event. Post a picture of you and your whole team on your webpage, then ask your team members to send their friends to the team page to donate. It's fun to give the team a name to create buzz around the event.

Choosing the Best Venue

You'll want to assess your venue carefully. A school's running track is a great option. Avoid uncomfortable surfaces such as a blacktop road in the middle of a hot day or a crushed gravel road (yes, this has happened). Our Barefoot Mile director coaches those who organize the walks, ensuring the host tests the venue by walking it barefoot beforehand (so that the conditions don't come as a shock).

Whatever you decide to do, wherever you decide to do it, we recommend telling potential supporters that every step they take raises funds to help JOY rescue more girls. When JOY International has funds, girls are rescued. It's that simple. The more funds we receive, the more girls we can rescue.

Appendix D

Write Your Legislators

*Action without vision is only passing time, vision without action
is merely day dreaming, but vision with action can change the world.*
NELSON MANDELA

"Jeff, what's the answer? How do we stop this? Child traffickers
are operating in my city. How do I stop this from happening?
Is it possible?"

The woman stared at me, genuinely concerned for her city. She
had just heard my presentation at the national school safety symposium at which John-Michael and Ellen Keyes of the I Luv U Guys
Foundation had invited me to speak. I answered her in two words:
mandatory sentencing. Mandatory sentencing is a key factor to
ending this scourge. When I'm asked what the answer might be to
ending child abuse, my answer is unequivocal.

Mandatory Sentencing

Mandatory sentencing is the legal answer to trafficking. We *must*
stop plea bargaining with criminals who abuse children.

Ultimately, in the United States the problem exists within the
U.S. legal system. The perpetrators plea bargain with the prosecutors, so the court indulges them with various options:

- "If you go to these classes, we'll knock this many months off your sentence."
- "If you spend plenty of money on a lawyer we approve of, we'll lower your sentence."
- "If you admit you've been a 'bad boy,' we'll lower your sentence."
- "If you plead guilty to a misdemeanor rather than the actual felony you perpetrated, we'll take it into account and lighten your sentence."

We have to eliminate any type of plea bargaining! If you're caught trafficking a child or any human being, you should go to prison for at least ten to twenty years (or more) with no possibility of parole.

Is there a model for this approach anywhere in the world, and if so, is it effective? Yes, there is, and yes, it *is* highly effective. Sweden is perhaps the only country in the world where trafficking has virtually been eradicated. If you're caught trafficking humans in Sweden, you *will* serve a prison sentence. The person being trafficked, whether an adult or a minor, is not arrested but rather justly treated as a victim. Traffickers are treated as criminals. Pedophiles who are caught paying to have sex with underage children are charged with rape and go to prison. Offenders are not treated as customers paying for a service but as criminals who rape children.

I want to see the same happen around the world—human traffickers, brothel owners, pimps, pedophiles, and abusers of children arrested, charged, and sentenced for their crimes. In my opinion plea bargaining, suspended sentences, and fines are a diabolical travesty of justice. I readily confess that this blatant indulgence of criminals angers me deeply.

On a positive note, the woman at the symposium who had asked me, "How do I stop this from happening?" became the attorney general of Colorado a year or two after this. In November 2017, she prosecuted a child trafficker and procured the longest prison sentence in history for a child trafficker—472 years![1] Did my answer to her question help with this? I don't know for sure, but I believe it helped in some way.

Please take the time to write your state legislator and state attorney general to advocate for mandatory sentencing. For help doing this, e-mail info@joy.org, or see the sample letter below.

Sample Letter to Advocate for Mandatory Sentencing

One of the most important factors in fighting sex trafficking is mandatory sentencing of perpetrators. Use the sample letter below to send to legislators, and advocate for mandatory sentencing for sex traffickers and their clients.

[month, day, year]

The Honorable [first and last name]
[room number], State Capitol
[city, state, zip code]

RE: Mandatory sentencing for sex traffickers

Dear [Assembly Member/Senator] [last name]:

My name is [your first and last name], and I am a citizen who resides in your district.

I am writing to express my concerns regarding the increasing growth of human sex trafficking in our state/city and advocate for mandatory sentencing of traffickers, pimps, and pedophiles (clients) who sell or buy sexual services of underage minors.

Despite public perception, human slavery is still a viable trade in our communities. The average age of entry into the sex trade in the United State is twelve to fourteen years old. These children are sold for the financial gain of traffickers and the perversion of buyers.

As a society and in our laws, we have only in the past decade begun to recognize the victimization of children and women trapped in human trafficking. Our nation formally recognized the crime of human trafficking in 2000 with the passage of the U.S. Trafficking Victims Protection Act (TVPA).

However, to truly protect both victims and potential victims, mandatory sentencing is a non-negotiable. Too many times traffickers and buyers are caught but then soon released through plea bargaining. Or their sentence is lightened to little or even no time in jail/prison. The commercial sexual exploitation of children is a crime in the United States and should be treated like one.

Without mandatory sentencing, the buying and selling of minors holds no risks for these men and women. Plea bargaining, suspended sentences, and fines are a diabolical travesty of justice.

This issue has become very personal for me as I have come to understand the travesty of this widespread issue. Sex trafficking is now the second-largest and fastest-growing crime industry in the world. I cannot turn a blind eye to this, knowing what I now know.

I ask that you please vote for mandatory sentencing for traffickers and buyers and use your platform to tell others about this vital key to fighting this epidemic.

Thank you for your leadership to protect victims and potential victims of human trafficking.

Sincerely,

[sign your first and last name]

[your first and last name printed]
[your street address]
[your city, state, zip code]

Notes

Introduction: In the Red-Light District

1. Mahesh Nair, "The Great Indian Head Bobble," CNN, January 23, 2012, travel.cnn.com/mumbai/life/great-indian-head-bobble-054242 (accessed March 8, 2018).

Chapter 2: A Nice Jewish Boy

1. "Yeshua" is the Hebrew form of "Jesus." As a Messianic Jew, I prefer to use this form.

Chapter 3: A Clown Is Born

1. "Micromagic, or close-up magic or table magic, is stage magic performed in an intimate setting usually no more than ten feet (three meters) from one's audience and is usually performed while sitting at a table." Mark Wilson, *Mark Wilson's Complete Course in Magic* (Philadelphia: Courage Books, 1988), 17–171.
2. Floyd Shaffer in "A Clown, for Christ's Sake," *Weekly World News*, August 25, 1981.

Chapter 5: Rich Kid, Poor Kid

1. Dictionary.com, s.v. "scheduled caste," www.dictionary.com/browse/scheduled-caste, (in India) the official name given to the lower castes that are now protected by the government and offered special concessions.

Chapter 7: Seven Seconds of Terror

1. "Commercial Sexual Exploitation of Children," Office of Juvenile Justice and Delinquency Prevention, Department of Justice, www.ojjdp.gov/programs/csec_program.html (accessed March 9, 2018).
2. Exodus Cry, *Intervention Training Manual* (Kansas City, MO: Exodus Cry, 2015). Used and adapted with permission.

Chapter 10: Fifty Failures

1. Zubair Ahmed, "Bombay's Crack 'Encounter' Police," BBC, June 9, 2004, news.bbc.co.uk/2/hi/south_asia/3786645.stm (accessed March 5, 2018).

Chapter 16: In Our Own Backyard

1. "Trafficking in Persons Report 2017," U.S. Department of State, www.state.gov/documents/organization/271339.pdf (accessed March 8, 2018).
2. Rachel Swaner, Melissa Labriola, Michael Rempel, Allyson Walker, and Joseph Spadafore, "Youth Involvement in the Sex Trade: A National Study," Center for Court Innovation, June 2016, viii, www.ncjrs.gov/pdffiles1/ojjdp/grants/249952.pdf?ed2f26df2d9c416fbddddd2330a778c6=jaccjssvkj-jdvsadwa (accessed March 8, 2018).
3. Ibid., xiii. In recent years it was reported that some 200,000 to 300,000 children had been forced into the sex trade in America and that the average age of girls initiated into the industry was twelve or thirteen. These numbers are now widely thought to be inflated. A recent report indicates that numbers may be between 9,000 and 10,000, with a high estimate of 21,000, and an average entry age of about sixteen. See Glenn Kessler, "New Study: Far Fewer Juveniles Engaged in Sex Trade Than Previously Estimated," July 21, 2016, *Washington Post*, www.washingtonpost.com/news/fact-checker/wp/2016/07/21/new-study-juveniles-engaged-in-sex-trade-much-lower-than-previously-estimated/?utm_term=.19cb575e8c69 (accessed March 12, 2018).

Chapter 17: A Lucrative Trade

1. Melissa Farley, "QuickFacts," Prostitution Research and Education, 2016, prostitutionresearch.com/category/quickfacts (accessed March 5, 2018).

Chapter 18: After a Rescue

1. "FBI Rescues 149 Children, Arrests 153 in Operation Targeting Sex-Traffickers," Behind the News, October 14, 2015, btnews.online/2015/10/14/watch-fbi-rescues-149-children-arrests-153-in-operation-targeting-sex-traffickers (accessed March 8, 2018).
2. *The Day My God Died*, documentary, Andrew Levine Productions, 2003.

Chapter 20: A Heart That Weeps

1. Adapted from Loren Eiseley, *The Star Thrower* (Wilmington, MA: Mariner, 1979), 169–85.

Chapter 21: Abolitionist

1. "Huckleberry Finn vocab chapter 4–7," Quizlet, quizlet.com/42512851/huckleberry-finn-vocab-chapter-4-7-flash-cards (accessed March 8, 2018).
2. The Underground Railroad was a vast network of secret routes and safe houses used by nineteenth-century enslaved people of African descent in the United States in efforts to escape to free states and Canada with the aid of abolitionists and allies who were sympathetic to their cause.
3. Harriet Tubman, Biography, www.biography.com/people/harriet-tubman-9511430 (accessed March 8, 2018).
4. Henry Louis Gates, Jr., "How Many Slaves Landed in the U.S.?" PBS, www.pbs.org/wnet/african-americans-many-rivers-to-cross/history/how-many-slaves-landed-in-the-us (accessed March 8, 2018).
5. "What Is Human Trafficking?" Exodus Cry, exoduscry.com/about/human-trafficking (accessed March 8, 2018).
6. "ILO Says Forced Labour Generates Annual Profits of U.S. $150 billion," International-al Labour Organization, May 20, 2014, www.ilo.org/global/about-the-ilo/newsroom/news/WCMS_243201/lang--en/index.htm (accessed March 5, 2018).
7. "Human Trafficking Syndicates More Organized and Increasing Rapidly," Kuala Lumpur Post, April 25, 2013, www.kualalumpurpost.net/human-trafficking-syndicates-more-organised-and-increasing-rapidly (accessed March 8, 2018).
8. Lane Anderson, "Human Trafficking Is Fastest-Growing Crime in the World," Washington Post, January 9, 2015, www.washingtontimes.com/news/2015/jan/9/human-trafficking-is-fastest-growing-crime-in-the- (accessed March 8, 2018).

Chapter 22: The Right Word

1. I Love U Guys Foundation, www.iloveuguys.org.

Appendix B: A Little Child Shall Lead Them

1. Unfortunately, the bus ministry is no longer available to these children due to financial constraints.

Appendix D: Write Your Legislators

1. Travis Fedschun, "Colorado Child Sex Trafficker Sentenced to 472 Years in Prison," Fox News, November 22, 2017, www.foxnews.com/us/2017/11/22/colorado-child-sex-trafficker-sentenced-to-472-years-in-prison.html (accessed March 11, 2018).

INTERNATIONAL

THE PURPOSE OF JOY INTERNATIONAL is to be involved in or help coordinate the *rescue, restoration*, and *reintegration* of children exploited by the commercial sex industry as well as the *prevention* of such exploitation, domestically and internationally.

Rescue

We actively work with like-minded organizations in relevant geographic locations to rescue women and children from the commercial sex trade, freeing them from slavery and bondage. We partner with police, task forces, prosecutors, and nonprofit ministries to find and rescue captive children throughout the world and bring their captors to justice.

Restoration

JOY is committed to seeing those released from the sex industry healed emotionally, spiritually, mentally, and physically. We partner with safe houses and rehabilitation professionals to ensure the safety and care of these precious women and children as they walk the road to healing.

Reintegration

Our safe homes educate and train survivors in relevant schooling and job-placement courses, preparing them to reintegrate into society as healthy, educated, and trained adults. JOY also sponsors young women's continuing education costs, providing them an opportunity to go to university and end the poverty cycle in their lives.

Prevention

Demand, poverty, and lack of education are three of the driving forces behind the sexual exploitation of children around the world. We strive to educate vulnerable people groups about human trafficking by providing them with relevant information on traffickers' schemes, and we also provide food, clothing, and shoes to help ease the burden of poverty on families around the world. The best form of prevention is seeing a perpetrator put in prison; JOY is devoted to seeing perpetrators arrested, prosecuted, convicted, and imprisoned.

FOR ADDITIONAL INFORMATION

Please visit
www.joy.org or www.facebook.com/joy.org,
call 303-838-0880,
e-mail info@joy.org,
or write to
JOY International
P.O. Box 571
Conifer, CO 80433, U.S.A.